D1107557

# CITY OF THE GOLDEN 'FIFTIES

# CITY OF THE GOLDEN 'FIFTIES

*Pauline Jacobson*

UNIVERSITY OF CALIFORNIA PRESS
BERKELEY AND LOS ANGELES
1941

UNIVERSITY OF CALIFORNIA PRESS
BERKELEY, CALIFORNIA

CAMBRIDGE UNIVERSITY PRESS
LONDON, ENGLAND



PRINTED IN THE UNITED STATES OF AMERICA
BY THE UNIVERSITY OF CALIFORNIA PRESS

*For who loves me must have a*
*touch of earth;*
*The low sun makes the color.*

—Tennyson, *Lancelot and Elaine*

# Introduction

WHEN PAULINE JACOBSON *was at the University of California, she applied herself seriously to the study of philosophy, even to the endangering of her health. So she came to writing as a trained thinker, acquiring also from that application to the masters in the mental domain a high passion for form in composition. So scrupulous was she that her work was produced slowly and with much groaning of the spirit; though the reader is not conscious of the effort, for Pauline had mastery of the difficult* ars celare artem.

*That great editor, Fremont Older, recognized Pauline's unusual ability from the start of her work on the old* Bulletin, *and carefully picked out for interviews by her the San Francisco personalities best designed to challenge her interest and evoke from her what may be called the heat of friction. From her ivory tower she would descend to make a divekeeper turn himself inside out, and when she put the man's soul on paper, Older had a masterpiece.*

*In the interviewing field of the older days one finds her local peer only in Ashton Stevens.*

*There was an exceptional group of good writers on the* Bulletin *of Pauline's time, good writers in prose and verse. Mention may be made of Ralph E. Renaud, Virginia Brastow, W. O. McGeehan, John Taylor Waldorf, Lowell Otus Reese, and John Hamilton Gilmour. These all recognized the individual quality of her work, although, characteristically enough, they seldom paid her compliments. Pauline was avid of encouragement, not of praise; and she came to understand that the hard-boiled attitude of her colleagues was a pose concealing a hearty admiration for a great craftsman. Those who are still living could readily recall some of those Jacobson interviews.*

*Emphasis has been placed on her success as an interviewer because that was her weekly assignment for a long time; her series on the colorful early days came later, and though the careful observance of a pattern in writing is observable, it may be doubted if this work "extended" her to the same breadth of treatment as did the inspiring clash of personalities in her* vis-à-vis *probing of a James W. Coffroth or an Eddie Graney.*

*Pauline was by no means an omnivorous reader, but what books she read she digested, to the strengthening of an intellect which conditioned her approach to all she wrote.*

*Another influence, known only to her intimate friends, was her early indoctrination in the orthodox Jewish faith. The sobriety that lay at the basis of her character was main-*

*tained and humanized by her reverence for the Torah and, so to speak, by the seven-branched candlestick of the tabernacle.*

*Her sense of humor was keen, and her laugh was one of merriment. Her judgments were ever on the sweet level of charity, though she penetrated foibles and worse than foibles so unerringly that she might have been excused for a* saeva indignatio. *She simply did not have anything of the sort.*

*Pauline's death left many of us with a sense of loneliness. We have not stopped missing her.*

*These are inadequate comments on a wonderful woman. My wife, who loved Pauline and was with her as often as possible when the ultimate shadow began to deepen, should be writing this tribute.*

EDWARD F. O'DAY

# Author's Preface

THE FREE SPIRIT *that still lives in San Francisco, and is remarked by visitors from all over the world, represents a double heritage: from the Spanish colonials, hospitality, love of gaiety and display, and a little "Mañana, mañana" with which we temper the haste of a commercial civilization; from the pioneers, a willingness to take men as we find them, an unbounded belief in human capacity for great things, and a faith in human capacity for good things. For this last, I fear the city's leaders of pioneer days have lacked their due. But indeed we owe them much for the indulgent practicality with which they sought to introduce order and culture to the hit-or-miss population attracted by the Gold Rush.*

*The pioneers had recourse not so much to laws and prohibitions as to standards. They went on the principle that men tend to choose the best if the best is often and consistently presented to them. They did not stamp out the saloons; they sought instead to substitute for low drinking places bars refined in tone, decorated with works of art and conducted with decorum. To counteract the evils of the gambling dens, they fostered theaters and cherished the actor as a contributor to the public good. Even to civic enterprises in which no moral problem was involved they brought something more than the stark desire to meet an issue; the frequent and desperate necessity of fighting fires they always treated as a sport and passion.*

*In preparing these sketches of their Golden City, I have not attempted to write a history, but rather to recapture the attitudes of a life that began in 1849 and lasted until San Francisco became—with the widening of Kearny Street in 1864 and the drift of business toward Market Street—a city of the Gilded Age. The "Golden 'Fifties" cover a little more time than the term would strictly allow.*

*The traditional generosity of San Francisco makes it impossible for me to acknowledge a debt of gratitude to any particular person. From unexpected quarters, from friends and strangers alike,—a list too long to attempt,—came valuable information and original documents to my assistance. To all the city, to an appreciative audience for encouragement, I owe a debt of thanks.*

*These sketches first appeared as a weekly Saturday feature of the San Francisco* Bulletin *from March, 1916, to August, 1917. That they now assume book form is due, first of all, to the publisher and editor of that newspaper.*

PAULINE JACOBSON

# Editor's Preface

POSSIBLY THIS BOOK *requires some explanation; but certainly no apology. To the skeptic who flips it open and says, "Oh, another hodgepodge of early Californiana," the adequate reply is the book itself; let him read it, he will change his tune. He will find that it has unity, coherence, and emphasis, because its author was a person of decided character with an attitude of her own toward persons and events. She was no mere recorder, but always an interpreter.*

*A slightly more extended answer is indicated here for him who says, "What? A book about old San Francisco, and a university press book at that, without footnotes, appendixes, and bibliography?" The manuscript certainly offered many a temptation to an editor. So many things have changed, or moved, or disappeared entirely, since the sketches were first written in 1916–17, and rewritten before the author's death in 1928! Shouldn't the present-day reader be warned not to attempt a pilgrimage to the Bank Ex-*

*change? Told where to hunt for the Coras' weeping-willow headstone? Advised what books to consult for other, and contrary, opinions of the Vigilance Committees, their works and pomps? Urged to turn from the author's mention of Lola Montez in Paris to the dramatic account of* le duel Dujarier *in Fouquier's* Causes Célèbres, *where the original French of Dujarier's note to his darling Lola is interestingly at variance with the Victorian English of the translation in Lola's* Autobiography? *Shouldn't the unlabeled quotations be tracked down, and all quotations, dates, and names be verified?*

*No; for our author, as she herself says, "has not attempted to write a history, but rather to recapture the attitudes of a life." She views that life in her own way; other people's ways should not be permitted to interfere. She writes about it so that the old scenes have an air of melodrama played seriously; another atmosphere should not be suggested. And this last is why the book has no pictures. Photographs would have reduced the people in it to ordinary life size, and half their attraction is in their being a little bigger than that. Contemporary drawings wouldn't do; they are stiff and lifeless, or, if animated, are frankly caricatures. A commission to a modern artist would no doubt have produced good pictures; but then there would have been another view of things than the author's own. The word-pictures of the text must suffice; as, in fact, they do.*

HAROLD A. SMALL

# Contents

# CITY OF THE GOLDEN 'FIFTIES

# 1

# She, the Seventh

THAT FIRE of April, 1906, was a "she." The firemen all say: *"She* jumped," *"She* crossed," "There *she* was a-comin' down the street." She was multiple. It was not one but fifty fires that stirred the city from sleep before seven that morning—fifty dancing witches with abandoned fire-glow hair. Whipped together by a furious wind, they swelled and raged hour after monstrous hour, until by evening there was one vast conflagration reeling through the city, with breath so hot as even to set ablaze newspapers lying the width of a street away. The firemen got water where they could: from the mains as it was going into the sewers, from the old cisterns, from tugboats and private boats, even salt water from the Bay. They couldn't tell one day from another. It was darkness and light; that was all they knew. All the sleep they had was a few minutes standing in some doorway. They snatched a mouthful of food or drink, with one hand always on the pipe line. They saved half the city.

The fire of April, 1906, was "She, the Seventh." In the eighteen months between December, 1849, and June, 1851, San Francisco had six great fires. From the fifth fire many fled, never to return, declaring the city doomed. But there were others of greater vision and courage who remained, saying that with her wonderful resources nothing could stop San Francisco from becoming a great city. After the sixth fire, they rebuilt with brick and stone. They put up walls that were two and three feet thick, with double iron doors and shutters. They organized a superb volunteer fire department. They installed huge water tanks that could flood a building from top to bottom, and enlarged their public water cisterns. It was these tanks and cisterns that helped to save San Francisco from total destruction a half century later.

When "She, the Seventh" was over, the once joyous, brilliant, teeming downtown district lay like a city centuries dead—acres and acres of stillness, of blinding white ashes and ruins, of streets impassable because of heaped-up mounds of fallen bricks and mortar and twisted iron. Not a sound, no sign of life, save an occasional pedestrian or a hack with wheels resounding loudly over the broken pavements; or a saloon man reduced to sweet-soda selling behind an improvised bar of empty packing boxes erected in the shadow of some ruin. At night complete darkness, save for the light of stars or the moon, or the faint rays from the lone shack of some guard watching over the treasure vault of a bank.

But out of those waste spaces arose a wonderful, modern metropolis of skyscrapers, luxurious hotels and apartment houses, theaters and cafés brilliant with light and ringing with music. Those acres of stillness gave way to the swish of automobiles and taxicabs, and the pound and clang of the big "pay-as-you-enter" cars. Under an impassable hill the city has attained the metropolitan glory of a subway,—oh, nothing so dark and deep and long as in New York,—two blocks long only, and only two flights steep, but quite, notwithstanding, with the metropolitan thrill. And where once a penny offered as change would have been an insult, the people have learned, through cafeterias, Eastern "penny papers," and department stores, to endure, nay, even to expect and demand it, as is the way of the old cities that never knew a birth in gold.

Not much more than sixty years before, San Francisco billowed in sand hills; the people came by perilous journey in prairie schooners across the continent, or by tedious slow passage round the Horn; railroads were undreamed of; pans of gold dust stood on every counter, and the smallest coin of exchange was ten cents. Gone is that Golden City, swept away in the mad revel of "She, the Seventh." Only a few blocks remain, bounded by Montgomery and Sansome, Jackson and Washington streets, and a single public house, the Bank Exchange.

# 2

# A Fire-defying Landmark

IN THE downtown district the one link between the age of iron and the days of gold is the Bank Exchange, a saloon on the ground floor of the Montgomery Block at the corner of Washington and Montgomery streets. Untouched, the Bank Exchange remains today as when its swinging doors first opened in 1853. Everything in it came round the Horn: the marble flagging; the enormous solid mahogany free-lunch table; the mahogany bar, its edges rubbed smooth by the elbows of countless drinkers, its counter worn by dice rattled at twenty gold dollars a throw; the mirror and the mahogany glass-racks; the engravings of scenes of the French Revolution, mildewed with age, yet by connoisseurs reckoned worth $1500, and the two prints in the back room, of the House of Commons and House of Lords.

The Montgomery Block was built on piles, for the Bay came up to Montgomery Street then; at high tides, when it was being built, to the delight of the small boys of Telegraph Hill the water rose so far that they could float rafts among the piling. Sansome, the block below, solid today with business buildings, was part of the Bay, crowded with vessels, often to four and five hundred. In those days Montgomery was not graded and the sidewalks ended at California in slippery sand. Kearny, the block above, was paved with a crazy assortment of scraps and litter—old barrel staves, rusty stove tops, broken kegs, hatch covers from old ships. Livery stables, and the cheaper saloons and restaurants, were on Kearny.

In the city that rose from the ashes of the sixth great fire the Montgomery Block was the most superb and imposing of all. Evidence of its old iron shutters and doors can still be seen at the Bank Exchange. Sometime in the 'nineties the iron balcony which extended along the front was torn away. After the fire of 1906 ten of the faces of early pioneers cut in a frieze above the first story were removed to the museum in Golden Gate Park, to make room for a cigar store; the faces which remain look down upon the street, little changed by time.

The life and activity of the city centered at Washington and Montgomery. Within the radius of a few blocks from this corner were all the first-class business houses, banks, express offices, theaters, and many of the engine houses, saloons, and gambling and dance halls. On every counter of the business houses stood pans of gold dust. All night long sounded the strains of music, the rattle of ivory chips, the clink of gold and silver on the tables of faro, roulette, poker, and monte. The El Dorado, the finest gambling hall of its day, was a block from the Bank Exchange, overlooking the Plaza—now Portsmouth Square. Facing the Plaza were many of the French restaurants, hotels, and lodging houses, and a few blocks beyond were the aristocratic boardinghouses.

Diagonally across from the Bank Exchange, and within a stone's throw, was Maguire's Opera House, on Washington Street. In Merchant Alley, which flanks the Montgomery Block to the south, was the old *Bulletin* office at the time when its editor, James King of William, was shot by Casey. Half a block beyond, on Clay, was the Blue Wing saloon, where Charles Cora was drinking when called to his fatal encounter with Colonel Richardson. In the Montgomery Block James King died; the Block was filled with law offices, and most of the heads of firms and their clerks, for lack of other accommodation, slept in offices and stores. As Casey and Cora were being hanged at the headquarters of the Vigilantes at Front and Sacramento streets, the immense funeral procession of James King was passing along Washington and Montgomery. No parade of any note but passed this corner.

The Bank Exchange, center of all, was a gentleman's saloon, and drinks were never less than two bits. Barry and Patten were the pioneers of the "gentleman's saloon" as an institution. They were from New England and themselves were gentlemen. No other place in the world, perhaps, for the size of its population, had as many drinking places as San Francisco. They were for the most part low dives hung with lewd pictures, the resort of roughs and criminals, where bad liquor was sold. It was after the sixth fire that Barry and Patten opened their saloon in the Brannan Building on Montgomery. The walls were hung with chaste oil paintings. The wines and liquors were of the finest, the free lunch of the best. Gambling was excluded; instead, the upstairs was fitted out with an elaborate billiard parlor. Some other establishments of like character sprang up. The Bank Exchange was one, its proprietors the Parker Brothers, of the Astor House, New York. It surpassed all others in splendor; its oil paintings alone were worth $100,000. Years later, one of them, "Samson and Delilah," was sold to Milton S. Latham for $10,500. He disposed of it later to Haquette, of the Palace of Arts.

Until 1862 the leading brokers transacted their business in the Bank Exchange. Here came also the leading bankers and merchants, the chief of the Fire Department, the leading members of the bench and bar, the sea captains, and the army and navy officers, among them Lieutenant Derby, whose *Phoenixiana* is said to have been the inspiration of Mark Twain's later humor. Here Governor Foote, who, in behalf of Bella Cora, interceded to have Colonel Baker defend Cora, was converted from the side of Law and Order to the opposition, the Vigilantes. One of the Parkers was a member of the Vigilance Committee, and during the terrible excitement the Bank Exchange was crowded to the doors. Governor Foote was not a drinking man, but, with his volatile temperament, he fell in with the crowd that surged to the bar—and went away a lifelong supporter of the Vigilantes.

With the widening of Kearny Street and the exodus toward Market, the glory of the Bank Exchange as a center of the early life vanished. It still continued to make money, however, until the City Hall was moved to McAllister Street and only the Hall of Justice was left. Then it went under the hammer. It was at this time that the painting of "Samson and Delilah" was sold. That was not a great painting, but around it clustered so many associations of pioneer days that the wealthiest men of the town bid for its possession.

For three months the Bank Exchange stood idle. Then Brown, who had acquired Sam Sample's place, together with "Little" Perkins, Garcia's bartender, took it over. The Bank Exchange once more "rattled with money," for Perkins took much of Garcia's trade. But "Little" Perkins died and Brown sought out Duncan Nicol as partner.

Then once more the Bank Exchange was forgotten. The fire of 1906 made of it the only public house remaining of the days of old. Duncan Nicol, now the proprietor, the only public host alive of the old "Ambrosial Path," continued to dispense the traditional hospitality; but only a few faithful came to recall the vanished glories.

To "plagiarize" from my own article, written in the *Bulletin* under date of May 4th, 1912:

"Dwarfed now is that block into insignificance by the steel-structural skyscrapers built in the wisdom of the seventh fire. Sleepy even at noon is the once active corner. At spasmodic intervals an antiquated car crawls past the Bank Exchange, waking the stillness by the noisy jerk of its painful travel over the worn track. By night it is as deserted as a village byway.

"The Bank Exchange is a gentlemen's saloon still. Duncan will have no rough element. Recently he warned a millionaire who was spending money freely, but had grown abusive, that he wanted none of his money if he couldn't keep a quiet tongue in his head. The same quality of 1853 holds with the liquors and wine, although, since the fire, the price on straight drinks has been reduced a 'bit.' Thirty-year-old brandy is to be had, and Duncan's 'Pisco Punch' is famed as in the old days."

The secret of Duncan's success in mixed drinks, Johnny, the little ex-barber, confides in whispered admiration: "E-v-e-r-y one of them is mixed the same. I had nine of them punches and e-v-e-r-y one of them was mixed the same. If you came in here for THIRTY-FIVE YEARS, e-v-e-r-y one would be mixed the same. Watch him!"

Duncan, oblivious and intent upon his work, clad in a handsomely frogged, spotless, white linen coat, his eyeglasses hung behind one ear as a bookkeeper holds his pen, his white hair cropped close, his smooth-shaven face pink with health, is standing behind his shining bar, its tall vases filled with roses from his garden. With hands trembling with the years, yet measuring with the nicety of an apothecary, he is mixing several ingredients in a thin cut glass.

"See," coaches Johnny, "he is squeezing a f-r-e-s-h lemon. In the bars uptown they have the lemon juice already prepared, which leaves a bitter taste after drinking. And Duncan n-e-v-e-r uses any of them effervescent waters," with a contemptuous intonation for the cheaper art of the uptown bars; "he always uses distilled water."

Here in fine camaraderie are mingled life's successes and life's failures. Johnny quotes Shakespeare in his high, thin, childlike voice. Johnny is short and stout, with a bristling white mustache, little deft fingers, little feet that scarcely reach the floor, and the heart of youth within him. He came in the early 'fifties, and as newsboy and messenger, and finally barber, never worked elsewhere than at his beloved corner of Washington and Montgomery. As a newsboy, years ago, he never missed a night at the theater. So conversant did he thus become with Shakespeare that if the actors omitted a line he yelled corrections from his seat in the gallery.

Duncan's is busiest at noon, now, and at six o'clock; the officials come from the Federal buildings, the lawyers, judges, and reporters from the Hall of Justice. There is a steady, quiet clink of glass, a quiet rattle of dice. Punctual as clockwork, at certain set hours, come the old-timers who patronized the Bank Exchange sixty years ago and who take a drink nowhere else.

In the back room where hundreds of thousands of dollars have changed hands overnight, in stock deals, the "Cabinet" congregates—a group of aging men filled with the wit and spirit which made the old Bohemian Club famous. No dues are asked, no other qualification is demanded for membership than the applicant's assertion that he remembers when the Bay came up to Montgomery Street—indeed, with his own eyes saw the water there.

In this back room, its walls decorated with old prints, and including among its essential furniture a table covered with antiquated reference books, the "Cabinet," seated in armchairs that came round the Horn, and toasting their feet at Duncan's gas stove, may be seen the livelong day and till half-past ten of a night, discussing, as of the vital present, issues a half-century dead.

They are perennial experts on literary matters.

"So," delightedly, from the President, "they have got as far as 'simple' in the Oxford Dictionary. I had HEARD they had got as far as the M's."

" 'The dictionary,' " quotes the Secretary, " 'is a breeder of ignorance.... It opens its doors with tavernlike hospitality to all forms of speech.' "

The President is an adherent of the Baconian theory. But the Secretary, in a satirical article, has set forth, with the aid of a "Baconian cipher," that the sonnets of Shakespeare were written by Robert Browning, Theodore Roosevelt, and Lord Byron.

The officers are self-appointed, the President for his masterly look and his talent for ruling. The Secretary's most arduous task, up to date, has been to acknowledge receipt of some luscious fruit from the ranch of a nonresident member.

It is ten o'clock. Duncan's is a day saloon now, but he stretches the time leniently for the "club." His fine old face appears in the doorway, and with a gentle smile he chides, "Come now, all, for the doch-an-dorrach."

Duncan was bartender in the old days for the youngest Parker brother in the Parker House across the street. He maintains unmarred the spirit of those historic days. Of life's failures he never questions how much they eat of the free lunch, how few drinks they buy, how long they linger in the warmth and companionship of the back room.

Again the turn of the wheel. Once more fortune smiles, this time gently radiant. The Bank Exchange has become a Temple of the Past. Duncan Nicol, faithful servitor in Montgomery Street this half century or more, is its high priest. To it come tourists from all over the world, as well as men and women from every part of the city—sons and daughters of pioneers, bringing their sons and daughters,—votaries all, to the Bank Exchange, the only public house remaining of the glamorous days of gold.

Gone, however, are the gas stove and the reference library, to make room for these modern votaries. Even Johnny, though hale and hearty, now seldom pilgrimages down.

"The ladies don't want us old fellows about," says Johnny, "when they come with their young men escorts."

Pish Tush protests, with a malignity quite foreign to his gentle nature, "They've chased us out!"

The Timeless One sighs.

# 3

# Pish Tush

"EVER SINCE the water came up this far and whiskey was two bits a drink, Montgomery has been a gentleman's street," declared Pish Tush grandiloquently, drawing himself up to the full of his stature in his pridefulness in the street.

Pish Tush is a Montgomery Street "lotus-eater." As drink or drug serves most men as an escape from the prison house of reality back to the Golden Age, so Montgomery Street serves Pish Tush. He was joyously attuned to the period of the "day of gold," its romance, its bold adventure, its seething excitement, its motley herding of men. With the present clanging age of steel, its noise and speed, man pitted against man in fierce competition, Pish Tush is completely out of sympathy. His refuge from stress of reality is in the somnolence of Montgomery, sleepy, even at noon, as if the spell of "mañana" were upon it.

Incidentally, Pish Tush is a claimant to the invention of the now classical dish called "Hangtown fry." Duncan Nicol credits the invention to Dennis, the cook at Collins & Wheeland's. Willard Girard, nephew of old Gobey, dates the dish back to the Comstock days, when a man about to be hanged, upon being asked what he wanted for his last breakfast, said, "Fried oysters, with scrambled eggs on top, and a few slices of bacon"; the victim's name and crime may long since have been forgotten, but he then and there gave to the world the recipe for a marvelous dish—a dish that is served today in every epicurean grill in San Francisco.

But this is the version I had from Pish Tush: "I was in Hangtown—which is Placerville. I had a couple of friends to dine at the hotel. So I butts into the kitchen and I says to the cook, 'Whatcher got to eat?' He says, 'Nothin' much but bacon an' eggs.' I says, 'What's in them cans on the shelf?' He says, 'Oysters.' I says, 'All right.' So I takes several slices of bacon and I chops 'em fine. Then I says to the cook, 'Put that in the pan and fry it." Then I takes the oysters from the can, half a dozen to each person, and I says, 'Put that in the pan.' Then, when the oysters are half done, I scramble the eggs, and I says, 'Put that in the pan, too, and when the eggs are done, serve!'

"I called it a Hangtown roast, but you can call it a Hangtown fry if you like. It took fine, and so when I returned to San Francisco I introduced it to the chef at Collins & Wheeland's, where it has been served as a famous dish ever since. Many's the time I served it to the bunch of us artists and writers who used to live on Montgomery Street—Frank Nankieville, Bob Davis, Pete Bigelow.

"The 'La Bohème' crowd had nothing on us. When we had a dollar we lived on the fat of the land, and when we hadn't a dime we didn't, like them, have to pawn our overcoats, because we didn't have any overcoats to pawn. Didn't need any in this climate."

"Pish Tush" is not a law-abiding appellation, but a sobriquet bestowed upon this person for his intemperate use of one interjection to express all his emotions. I may not give his real name; but you may know him any day that you see him on Montgomery Street. He always eats somewhere along the Street, he always sleeps within sight of the Street, his work and his recreation are never far from the Street. He is clad usually in fine tan covert cloth. His hair and beard are snow-white. He walks somewhat stooped, but his great breadth of shoulder and his height still bespeak his magnificent build. His face is refined and gentle in expression, with ready humor constantly crinkling his eyes to slits. His great shock of white hair and his flowing tie are after the fashion of Murger's heroes in *Scènes de la vie de Bohème.* His beard is cut in the prevailing fashion of the reign of Queen Elizabeth. His headgear is the San Francisco vogue of the fall of '49 and the spring of '50. His gait has the swaggering grace of the swashbucklers who sailed up and down the Pacific Coast before the advent of the padres.

With men he is the genial hail-fellow-well-met. Toward women he bears himself with all the courtly deference of a Sir Walter Raleigh. A single flaw mars the perfection of his homage; in speaking of the women who pilgrimage down, these days, to Duncan's Bank Exchange, *"Charming* ladies," he spits out, with a venom in that "charming" that is at variance with his gentle nature; *"charming* ladies, all of 'em. But they've chased us out—we've no place to meet and settle the affairs of state; they've chased us out. Where can we go?"

There are various simple ways of "spotting" a Montgomery Street lotus-eater. For one, get him talking of Kearny Street after it was widened.

Kearny Street before it was widened—a street of cheap saloons, cheap restaurants, and livery stables—was a thing to be loved and hallowed along with Montgomery Street when the latter was "a gully of mud filled in with rocks and chaparral from the hills."

Kearny Street after it was widened—a thing of concrete pavements, of modern stores and restaurants with handsome entrances and wide plate glass—is a vulgar hussy, beneath the serious consideration of a gentleman. In fact, I am informed on the excellent authority of one of these Montgomery Street lotus-eaters that even the women stenographers who have invaded their "gentleman's street" in the past few years are possessed of a surpassing dignity instantly marking them as superior to stenographers in any other part of the city. No breath of scandal dare touch them. Should the least reproach attach to their names, or to the name of any employer as the cause of it, both, through the outraged sentiment of the street, would be ostracized and forced to take up offices in thoroughfares less noble.

Yet another way is to mention Powell Street. Then even the gentle-minded Pish Tush sees red.

"If you want my opinion of Powell Street," says Pish Tush, "I'll tell you. It's a tarantula-twisting, tango-twirling street. No gentleman would be seen walking down Powell after seven o'clock in the evening. *Absolutely not!* It is a street of display. It is raw. It is a street that likes to show the dollar. Do you think I could be broke and get a drink on Powell Street? *Absolutely not!* But I could be broke six months on Montgomery Street and be drunk—like a gentleman—all the time.

"Take this 'No-Thank-You Club,'" he went on, warming to his task and running his long fingers through his long hair, while shaking it vigorously, like an angry lion its mane, into his eyes. "It never could have started on Montgomery Street. No gentleman ever says, 'No, thank you,' when another asks him to take a drink. He might say, 'Excuse me, I've had enough'; but if he said, 'No, thank you,' everybody would know he was a liar. On Montgomery Street, if a man has the price, he'll ask you to take a drink, and if he doesn't ask you, you know he hasn't the price. You may not have the price for six months, but he says, just the same, 'Here, Bill, come on; I've got the price'; he knows that the day you've got the price you'll do the same by him. But in Powell Street you've got to return the favor the next minute. That's no gentleman's way. In Powell Street they drink to show the dollar, but in Montgomery Street they drink for sociability."

"Now, if you're asking my opinion," said Johnny, "to my way of thinking," with a judicial air and a wry face, "this 'No-Thank-You Club' ain't no gentleman's style. Am I to go into a bar and see, here Jim, and here Harry, and Tom over there, and I go and take a drink by myself? That's no gentleman's style. A gentleman takes a drink just to pass the hour in sociability. The man who will belong to a 'No-Thank-You Club' is the kind of man that would go out to the Park and take a drink so nobody would see him. That w-o-u-l-d be a queer life, when everyone would go to the bar and take a drink by himself and walk out. It seems to me we'd be setting up a lot of cranks that way. There's no harm in drinking if you get argument and talk and sociability with it. But in them cafés uptown they've got too much of this hurrah-and-ragtime spirit."

"Ah, those days!" sighed the Timeless One. "Everybody was your friend! Everybody shook hands! But they drank wisely and well, slowly and with deliberation and dignity. Now they say, 'Spear another!' or 'Pin it on!' or 'Spill it!' Ugh! It is a desecration. The saloon was club, forum, theater, in those days," he went on. "It is a transient place these days. Nobody would think of writing a poem to his inamorata or reciting lines to his sweetheart or his mother in a saloon, as was the custom in the old days, I assure you."

Like the Faubourg St.-Germain to a French aristocrat, Washington and Montgomery is a stronghold to the Montgomery Street lotus-eater. To lotus-eat beyond that boundary is to stamp oneself hopelessly as of the bourgeois. The *ancien régime* knows only its Barry & Patten's, the Bank Exchange, the Parker House, and Frank Garcia's—in its heyday, before it moved farther uptown. To know too intimately Jimmy Gibbs's in Merchant Alley is to condemn oneself, out of one's own mouth, as being beyond the pale.

Jimmy Gibbs and his kind long since overthrew the first "gentlemen's cocktail route." Jimmy Gibbs believed in the sovereignty of the people. He believed you could keep a democratic place and still have class and that a "bit" was enough to charge for any drink.

Of these "bit saloons," the single exception not taboo for the old regime was Frank Garcia's place on Montgomery at Washington, familiarly known as "Frank's."

"Frank was king of bartenders—bar none," declares Johnny. "He came up from New Orleans as a first-class one, to the Bank Exchange. New Orleans turned out the finest bartenders in the country in them days. Frank's was a 'bit' place, as were the Snug, Squarza's, and Jimmy Gibbs's. Squarza was the first to introduce ravioli, and he had all kinds of punches in urns arranged all around the room, same as in a coffee house, and he turned the punches on from a faucet just like coffee. He had 'em all made up—all kinds, cold and warm punches, brandy punches, rum punches, whiskey punches. Frank was famous for his "Imperial" punch. It was made of Santa Cruz rum, which you may know is pretty strong rum; double quantity of lime juice; brandy double rich, topped off with champagne, a pint to each person."

A spirited rivalry existed between the different high-class places, not only in elegance of appointments and decorations, free lunch, and patronage, but also in the mystery of their blended drinks. The Parker House boasted of its apple toddy, and the painting of "Eugénie and Her Maids of Honor." Barry & Patten prided themselves on their "Excellent," an appetizing bitters, drunk from a wineglass like sherry. The Bank Exchange had its "Pisco Punch" and the painting of "Samson and Delilah." There was also a punch by the name of "Quirós," well advertised by Mark Twain in *Roughing It.*

Frank's was the first to introduce, in connection with a saloon, a café where the men could bring the ladies to dine. The saloon, with entrances from both Washington and Montgomery streets, had, in the words of Johnny, whose shop was next door, "thirty feet, all painted white, of mirrors that high from the floor [indicating a wainscoting halfway to the ceiling], a panel of mirror here, and next a panel with a painting. The room was all painted white except the bar, which was painted black and had a solid black-walnut top."

The entrance to the café was at the rear, by way of Jones Alley, through a picket gate, into a garden with flowers and trees where the birds sang. The café was fitted up to resemble a grape arbor, and the sides and ceiling were constructed from the deckhouse of an abandoned ship.

"Twenty-five dollars was not an unusual price for a breakfast for two at Frank's," said Johnny. "Many a time I've seen

Colonel Michael Hawkins pay seven dollars and a half for his breakfast at Frank's and then walk right across to the Bank Exchange and get a pousse café. He'd pay as high as five dollars for his cigars at a single meal. If two men came in to breakfast and one said, 'I'll pay for the breakfast and you for the cigars,' he'd be getting the better of it. Breakfast was two dollars and a half and the cigars would be a dollar and a half each."

Jones Alley is a dilapidated byway now, its narrow sidewalks and cobbled road broken and sunk into receptacles for stagnant pools from winter rains, its pavement cellar gratings, rusted and warped with the years, yawning on both sides of the wide back doorways of warehouses that still retain the iron fireproof shutters of the 'fifties.

Where once wealth and fashion tripped gaily through the picket gate to dine at Frank's in a grape arbor with the birds singing all about, there is now a cooper's shop. Where once was "thirty feet of panels and mirrors" there are the insets only—rough and dusty boards. A little remains of the deckhouse; the rest has been used up by the coopers, for hardwood. Since the great fire of 1906 the coopers have treasured their deckhouse relic reverently. They proudly point it out now to visitors as all that remains in witness of the days when Yerba Buena, the village, was converted overnight into a city.

# 4

# The Timeless One

THE TIMELESS ONE kisses his fingertips to modernism, lightly wafting it, with a graceful flick of the hands, to the winds. His watch he has discarded these many years. "What need have I of a watch?" he queries. "I never take account of time. What care I for the time—the time of today? The past! Ah, the past is like incense!"

His eyes glow with a faraway look, his voice vibrates with the intensity of youth. "The past affords an exquisite exhilaration that no earthly drug can give. The man who cannot live in the past has no poetry, no imagination, no sentiment." And he adds with a passionate fling, "He is a man without a soul! He is like the bricks in the Parrott Building"—meaning not the present-day structure by that name on Market Street, but the Parrott Building on Montgomery Street. The Montgomery Street lotus-eater does not go beyond the Street, even for his figures of speech.

Of an afternoon, the Timeless One, immaculately clad

in the frock coat of the 'fifties, sallies forth to lotus-eat where of old the promenade, between the hours of three and eight, swung up and down the west side of Montgomery Street, past the Parrott Building at California, and the Union Club, past Barry & Patten's and the Parker House, and across at Washington to the Bank Exchange and Frank Garcia's.

The frock coat of the 'fifties was cut high in the back and ornamented with buttons, with wide-slanting silk lapels verging to a double-breasted buttoned front, and a wide skirt flaring full all around and reaching below the knee. This fashion of the skirt served two purposes: by reaching below the knee the ungainly line where boot met trousers was hid, and the wide, full flare by contrast made the boot appear smaller.

The vanity of men in those days equaled, if it did not surpass, the vanity of women. The brief, careless, red-shirted fashion of the fall of '49 and the spring of '50 gave way to an unsurpassed elegance and formality in dress, despite the fact that, as Johnny expressed it, "the principal thing here in them days was boots."

"There was considerable mud here in '58," explained Johnny, "and everybody wore boots. Ordinary people wore boots—just boots, plain boots. Sports and fashionable people had their boots made to order, costing from twelve to fifteen dollars. They had 'em fitted as tight and small as possible for walking. The heel ran from three to four inches high and narrowed at the end to the size of a quarter."

"Boot, singular, I pray you," chided the Timeless One,

uplifting his palm to ward off the full force of the barbarism. "A gentleman never used the word 'boots,' plural. You do not say 'bootsblack,' but 'bootblack,' a word descended from the day when the gentleman used the word 'boot' never otherwise than in the singular. Trousers were fitted snugly over the instep, then, and held by an elastic underneath so as to hold them down, the better to display the boot in all its perfection. But no one wears a boot today," and he shook his head long and sadly.

"Ah, no!" sighed another lotus-eater. "Only one man I know wears a boot today. He is Maynard Dixon, and his grandfather was a pioneer."

This bit of news served to restore the Timeless One somewhat to his accustomed cheerfulness.

Nor should one use so vulgar a word as "dress" in designating the fashion of that period.

"Apparel! Apparel!" entreated the Timeless One. "A gentleman never speaks of 'dress.' "

With the frock coat, costing from forty to fifty dollars, went a ruffled shirt costing from twelve to twenty-five dollars. It had a high collar, about which the cravat was wound twice and tied in front in what the Timeless One assured me was "an ample bow, quite ample."

"But, I beseech you," he said, "do not use the word 'necktie'—'cravat' always. 'Necktie' was to hang a man, as at a 'necktie party,' which meant a lynching.

"Everything was quite ample in those days, I assure you," he went on. "The kerchief—not handkerchief, I entreat you—was ample, most ample, not small and insignificant as today. The watches were made of heavy gold, and were corpulent like the men who wore them; and the chain was made of heavy links of polished gold quartz.

"Never say 'vest,' I beg of you." Again his palm was uplifted to parry the vulgarism. (Johnny had been telling me of the wonderful "vests" of that period, all "velvet and embroidered.") "Waistcoat, waistcoat," corrected the Timeless One. "Nor did gentlemen wear velvet. The gentlemen wore waistcoats made of calfskin and fine black cloth, embroidered in fleurs-de-lis or forget-me-nots. Or the color was purple. That was for thoughts—yes, thoughts of the lady. He wore, also, her colors. The gentlemen were beaux, who did not try to outclass each other, as today, but only to outshine each other in the splendor and distinctiveness of their apparel."

As to canes, Johnny maintains that canes did not come in until a much later period. The Timeless One, however, asserts that he has in his possession a walking-stick used by Broderick—he of the Broderick-Terry duel.

"They did not carry canes foppishly, nor for assistance," said the Timeless One. "They carried them for dignity and ready to use in saluting each other, thus": unhooking an imaginary cane from his left forearm, he presented it forward, as a soldier would his saber, touched it with great military precision to his forehead, again with military precision to the front, and replaced it to hang gracefully again upon the left forearm.

The Timeless One differs also on the matter of gloves. Barry and Patten, in their book, *The Spring of '50,* relating the story of the Great Unknown, speak of his faultless gloves of mode.

"No gentleman wore gloves," emphatically asserted the Timeless One. "A glove interfered with ready action, and a gentleman held himself at all times ready to draw a bowie knife in defense of a woman's honor."

And did gentlemen wear silk socks?

"Silk socks! Never! A pioneer would turn in his grave if he saw the socks the so-called gentleman of today wears. They wore white socks, for dyes had not yet come in. They wore them for comfort and for warmth and as a protection against the boot. They believed in keeping the head cool and the feet warm. It is quite the reverse now."

Spoke up another lotus-eater: "Nor would any man on Montgomery Street today wear what is worn on Powell Street. When my partner, a young man whom I imported from Powell Street, first saw me buying these white tucked shirts and plain pressed cravats, he said to me, 'Oh, don't buy those; they went out of style ten years ago.' But he's become converted. He doesn't buy any more of those flashy things he bought when I first had him in from Powell. He's beginning to see the greater dignity in the apparel of Montgomery. The men of Montgomery are more tailored and more pressed and more dignified in attire than the men of any other street. You see more Oxford grays—black with a little white—on Montgomery, and you see more long-tailed coats. And you don't see any of these green hats or checked suits and pearl-gray spats on Montgomery. Wherever you see green hats"—he came close and almost hissed it in the ear—"there you'll see wildcat schemes, jippo banks, and jippo contractors. You don't see any jippo banks, nor any buildings built by jippo contractors, on Montgomery Street."

"Nor would a gentleman wear these high silk hats with the straight brim that you see coming into vogue today," picked up the Timeless One. "They were worn by the butcher. You can see one of these oldtime butchers right now in the California Market, cutting meat and wearing his silk hat with the straight brim. The gentleman wore a silk hat with a wide, graceful roll, so as to display, underneath, the hair dressed and puffed and curled."

"All a barber knows how to do, these days," said Johnny, in a slightly contemptuous tone, "is to cut the hair pompadour or short. But a barber in them days had to know as much as a ladies' hairdresser does today. You had to know how to dress the hair and how to puff it. That is very difficult and a great deal of work—to puff the hair out. And men wore spit curls in them days, one on each side, the same as the ladies, and they had their hair curled just like the ladies, too."

From apparel they fell to talking of the Great Unknown. And Johnny's version of this odd character differs from that of Barry and Patten, who say the Great Unknown was an Englishman by birth who came to this country in infancy, was graduated from West Point, and took up commercial life; when he appeared suddenly in the midst of the Montgomery Street promenade, he was an old man but still with the elastic step of youth and of fine military bearing. Johnny, with a single skeptical shrug of his shoulders, dissipates the story in thin air. He asserts that the Great Unknown, whom no one took seriously, was a French pastry cook in a bawdyhouse. All are agreed, however, even Johnny, that the Great Unknown, expressive of the ultimate in the elegant fashion of that period, appeared each afternoon, punctual as clockwork, to stroll his hour in the promenade.

The whole town turned into the street at these hours, a gay and motley crowd—bankers, lawyers, judges, merchants, brokers, gamblers, all elegantly attired in frock coats, ruffled shirts, fancy waistcoats, tight-fitting trousers, and well-turned boots. Ladies of wealth and fashion tripped down from the exclusive quarters of California and Stockton; women came also from the half-world, and these, flaunting their finery, were brilliantly draped in Paisley shawls, then the height of the mode.

Mingling with the crowd, yet always apart, came the Great Unknown and Whispering Riley, and the Gutter Snipe—who foraged for his food in the gutter, yet was as disdainful of lesser men as even the Great Unknown. Always there was "Rosie," in filthy rags, yet who never failed, each day, to put a fresh rose in the lapel of his dirty coat. There was Topsy-Turvey, with her hat upside down and her coat inside out; of her it was said that she had gone insane over her lost fortune, gambled away in mining stocks. Also there was Emperor Norton, who had gone insane over his lost fortune—lost in grain deals,—and whom everyone saluted grandly, as befitted an emperor. Following upon his heels came Bummer and Lazarus, two mongrel dogs, who acquired their sustenance from the town—as did Emperor Norton—by right of imperial demand.

The promenade went by the blithe name of the "Ambrosial Path." It was mostly a parade of youth and hope and adventure, walking, as it were, in a rain of gold—the gold mined hardily along the American River and the Comstock, and as easily flung on the counters of Montgomery Street.

At dusk, mysteriously, as from nowhere, came the swallows, soaring in great flights overhead—as mysteriously to melt away with the thinning of the crowd and the lighting of the lamps.

From the Timeless One I have the story of Colonel Michael Hawkins' promenade along the Ambrosial Path: Colonel Hawkins was ever a splendid figure there. Whether or not he was buried in his spats, I don't know; he went to the almshouse wearing them, I am told, as he wore, also, his green four-in-hand, his pepper-and-salt trousers, and his cutaway coat, and carrying his cane with the same old swagger.

It was just after the fire of 1906, according to the Timeless One. The wreckers were blasting some condemned buildings. A police officer, stationed to warn off pedestrians, was startled to see the figure of a man dart through the doorway of a building about to fall. In a flash the policeman was after him. The man was bounding up the stairway. He disappeared into a room, to return as quickly, carrying something under his arm. The officer set upon him, almost throwing the man as well as himself into the street and reaching safety barely in time.

The man was Colonel Michael Hawkins. From under his arm, utterly unmindful of all else, he drew to view, with gloating eyes, an old silk plug hat, made with the graceful roll demanded by the gentlemen of the 'fifties. When the police officer realized that two lives had been risked for a plug hat more than fifty years out of date his fury was uncontrolled. Seizing the hat, he threw it down and trampled it. From that moment Colonel Michael Hawkins began visibly to pine away. The hat had been his "Open sesame" to the land of lotus-eating, where again he could be one with the elegance and wealth of the Ambrosial Path.

Colonel Hawkins had lost his fortune early in the 'seventies—in speculation, I am told, though he said he had been cheated out of it by a female cousin. The contention grew into an undying feud, and one day Hawkins fired a shot at his cousin when attending a party at her house. In his latter days the wrong became an obsession. No conversation of the Colonel's was ever quite complete that did not include the quarrel. In his pocket he always carried printed leaflets of his version of the affair, to be presented, free, to any who might lend an ear.

For some time Colonel Hawkins had an allowance from a relative; who, upon dying, however, failed to make any provision for the Colonel in his will. Hawkins was now upon the bounty of his friends. Drink was always to be had at Duncan's and food at the free-lunch counter, with not infrequent invitations to dine from one of the more well-to-do lotus-eaters.

So it was that the Timeless One, noting the grief of the old man over the loss of his silk hat, planned a surprise and a dinner. The son of some pioneer had given the Timeless One two silk plug hats of the fashion of the 'fifties, which had been found among the pioneer's effects. While the dinner was being prepared, the Timeless One brought forth one of these silk hats and graciously inquired whether it would be seemly to request the Colonel to accept it as a gift.

On the instant sight of the hat, youth leaped in the blood of the old man. His withered hand settled in trembling joy upon it. He placed it on his head, and began to preen himself in front of the long mirror. Something there was, however, not quite to his satisfaction. He tried on his gloves. But suddenly the critical eye of the old beau perceived the difficulty; there was needed the fine, graceful roll of a long frock coat—and he did not possess one. He bethought himself of his overcoat. Putting it on, he viewed himself up and down, coat, hat, gloves, in great glee, in the glass.

His thanks were profuse. Yet he hesitated, grew restive, and finally made bold to tell his host that he was an old man—his health was not good—he feared to be out late.

Would it be unseemly—in a gentleman—to beg to withdraw from dinner? The Timeless One smiled. He understood: the feeling found only too ready echo in his own heart. He slipped fifty cents into the old man's hand, and bade him hasten home before the shadows deepened.

Colonel Michael Hawkins made straight for the Ambrosial Path. His step was elastic, he held his head high. He was again the beau who took out every belle of note, the gay gallant, spending his money lavishly. Up and down he promenaded. Again, the gold shimmered behind every door. Again, overhead flew the swallows in great flights. Colonel Hawkins threw wide the swinging doors of the Bank Exchange, pausing a brief moment for a telling effect. The next, he strode across the marble flagstones to the bar. Upon the polished mahogany he flung, with the largesse of his onetime wealth, his single, solitary piece of silver.

It came to pass one day, upon the Colonel's entrance into the Bank Exchange, that Duncan was fain to shake his head. When the Colonel had been drunk, it was as a gentleman should be—gently so. But this time—"I knew it the instant I laid eyes on him," said Duncan, "I could tell he was drunk on *cheap* wine."

To the lotus-eaters of Montgomery Street Colonel Hawkins was already dead. It was not many months later that the almshouse claimed him for its own. There he really did die; and it was discovered that some unknown person had placed two hundred and fifty dollars at an undertaker's to save him from burial in the potter's field.

# 5

# Consider the Lilies

BUMMER AND LAZARUS, both, were mongrels of dark and sullied pedigree. Bummer was short-legged and shaggy, with a predominance of black Newfoundland, a well-poised head, an easy, graceless manner, a keen eye, strong, squarely set jowls, and a long, protruding under jaw which exposed his teeth and lent him a fierce and forbidding aspect. Yet he was as tender as he was valiant, as good as he was great.

Lazarus was plain cur. He had long legs, smooth fur, the face and throat of a fish, a slanting jaw, and a weak chin. He knew neither loyalty nor gratitude; he had neither courage nor ability for genuine effort. His single claim to distinction lay in a persistence in attaching himself to the mighty. He lived in the splendor, the glory, and by the bounty, of Bummer. He died a spectacular death, and though, to be sure, it contributed to the gaiety of the town, he was buried with great pomp. Bummer died in comparative obscurity, but his grave was watered with tears.

Bummer the mongrel rose to be king of the Ambrosial Path by the same virtue that resides in the lilies of the field. He knew neither home nor master, yet no petted lap dog fared more sumptuously. He sought no public honor, yet no blue-ribboned canine had greater public homage.

Bummer appeared on the street shortly after Bruno, his predecessor on the Ambrosial Path, had died of poisoning. Bummer, like Bruno, was homeless and without a master, a loafer, hence a "bummer"; thus in the curses and kicks of waiters he was christened. Bummer held the rather doubtful record of sustaining more kicks, with more poise and equanimity, than any other dog known. His was likewise the reputation, even from the beginning, of possessing almost superhuman intelligence.

His instincts led him always to the best. He had a regular beat—the east side of Montgomery between Sacramento and Washington. He was said to know every restaurateur and waiter on his beat, their comings and goings, and which place was the best for dinner, luncheon, or breakfast.

He never whined or begged for food. His plan for getting a meal showed wit and audacity. He would station himself outside the door of the restaurant and there take a critical survey of the diners as they went in. Almost legendary are the tales of Bummer's ability to read human character. His search was usually for two or three men who apparently were going to dine together and who gave evidence of openheartedness. After careful and cautious observation, having fixed upon his party, he followed leisurely behind it as a dog rightfully possessed by one of the men. At the table, whilst he kept an expectant eye on the food, he never betrayed too deep an anxiety to be fed. However famished he might be, he managed to assume the manner of the thoroughbred who knows that his master in due time will notice him. Each man, under the mistaken impression that the dog belonged to one of the others, fed Bummer royally, in deference to his supposed master. If his ruse was disclosed by the boot of some angry waiter, Bummer beat a hasty but dignified retreat.

Whether under kicks or pettings, the smiles or frowns of fortune, Bummer never abated a jot of his easy, graceless manner. Nor did he snatch so much as a bone to carry off against a rainy day. He relied upon concentration at the moment of practical need and his faith in the all-abundance of the Ambrosial Path to deliver him his next meal. And of such is the wisdom of the lily.

It was in 1861 that Bummer first came to the attention of the general public. An excavation was being made in the neighborhood of the Blue Wing saloon. In opening up the street, the men uncovered a small army of rats, which speedily overran both street and sidewalk. A mangy dog, with fierce teeth and forbidding countenance, sprang in among them, and slew so many, with such ease and might, that the crowd in wonderment began to inquire to whom this dog belonged.

The men along the Ambrosial Path, proud now of their acquaintance with Bummer, hastened forward, each trying to outdo the other in personal tales of the dog's superhuman qualities. So, in a day, Bummer became the public idol. The press devoted columns to his achievements. Jump, the cartoonist, extolled him in drawings. Every restaurant and saloon was thrown wide to him. But as Bummer the outcast had never maintained other than the highest dog standards, under his present agreeable change of fortune he found no occasion to alter either his beat or his manner.

One day, replete with food and honor, Bummer stood on the sidewalk, idly watching a poor, lean, and mangy dog being set upon by a larger dog. Suddenly he jumped fiercely into the fray and sent the aggressor flying down the street. The poor cur, one leg half bitten through, limped along the sidewalk after Bummer, and proceeded to scrape an acquaintance. He seemed to regard Bummer as his friend and protector. All day long, while Bummer ranged up and down the Ambrosial Path, glancing into people's faces to find a possible friend or lunch-eater, the lame cur followed confidently, and with evident interest in Bummer's activities. Bummer, on his part, regarded his sorry-looking protégé with pity not unmingled with contempt. Yet he seemed to feel the weight of his responsibility. At midnight the two dogs were discovered in a doorway. Bummer had given the sick dog the inner berth and was endeavoring with his body to keep him warm.

The next morning Bummer ranged his beat as usual, alone. He manifested, however, an astounding reversal of form, not only that day, but the next, and the next. For the first time, he was known to carry off choice bits of meat and disappear with them. The town sports began to wonder. They followed him. The trail led to a vacant lot, where, under a pile of empty boxes, the lame dog was discovered, safely and warmly ensconced. Here Bummer was seen to deposit the meat and, by sundry coaxings, entice the invalid to eat. Under this unremitting attention the nameless dog, cured of his lameness, soon appeared on the streets with him. Bummer continued to take good care of him, always giving him the lion's share of whatever turned up, so that the cur soon began to be the likelier-looking of the two. The town sports christened him Lazarus, seeing that he was raised from the dead by the power and the love of Bummer.

Not long afterward the town was outraged by the base ingratitude of Lazarus. Some evil-minded person had shot at Bummer and had wounded him in the leg. He began to mope and to slink into obscure corners, as sick dogs generally do. Lazarus instantly deserted him, returning, fawningly, only when Bummer was once more restored to his usual health and activity. Bummer forgot justice in pity. But Bummer's friends, the reporters, were not so lenient-minded; they denounced Lazarus in scathing terms.

And now it came to pass that dogs of all descriptions grew so numerous as to constitute a pest. To alleviate the city's condition a law was passed whereby any dog found roaming the streets unmuzzled was to be impounded, and, if unclaimed within twenty-four hours, shot. What, then, of Bummer and Lazarus, whom everybody owned, yet none?

Every professional man and every businessman of any significance hastened to place his signature on a mammoth petition to be presented to the Board of Supervisors for the relief of Bummer and Lazarus. When the Board convened, the two dogs were lying crouched at the threshold of the chambers. Some said the dogs were put there by reporters as a "cute dodge" to gain favorable action. Others stoutly maintained that Bummer gave every evidence of awareness not only of the nature of the petition, but also of the full danger lurking in the ordinance. Within an hour came the verdict. It surpassed all expectations. The two dogs, by an order under the hand and seal of the constituted authorities, were granted a special permit to roam the streets, unmuzzled and unmolested, the favored wards of the city. This privilege elevated them to the position of the city's guests.

Lazarus met his death in October, 1863, at a fire. Knickerbocker Five, Columbia Eleven, Washington Hose, and St. Francis Hook and Ladder each claimed the distinction of having run over and killed him.

The idea of a public funeral for Lazarus, it was said, emanated from the fertile brain of Ed Jump. The whole town, amid great gaiety, took part in the funeral rites. The skin was stuffed by Lorquin, the taxidermist, so skillfully that Lazarus, reposing on his carpet of velvet, seemed almost to speak. Many claimants contended for its possession. The Pioneer Association contended for it, the Board of Supervisors made overtures, and so did the proprietors of the saloons and restaurants along the Ambrosial Path. It finally went to Martin, the saloon man, who paid fifty dollars to the taxidermist and placed Lazarus on exhibition at his place.

Bummer mourned. The virtue went out of him. He attached himself to a likely-looking bull pup, who met his advances and received his bounty with disdain. Men lost their admiration for him. Bummer, sensitive, and quick as he had always been at reading human character, began for the first time in his life to whine and fawn for favor. He lost his self-respect. His easy, graceless manner disappeared. He grew careless of his personal appearance. He slunk away into corners, and finally into obscurity.

Thus two years passed. In September, 1865, the city learned, with consternation, that it still loved the Bummer whom for two years it had despised and ignored. The news that shocked the city read:

"Bummer is in a bad way. Last week a drunken bummer, who ought to roast at least in a place as hot as the upper Sacramento Valley for the term of his natural life, or longer, kicked poor old Bummer down a stairway on Montgomery Street and injured him so that he has never recovered and is not likely ever to recover. His body is swollen to twice its usual size and the poor fellow appears to be at death's door."

The offender, Faust Keller, was arrested and made to pay a fine of twenty-five dollars.

Each day, news of the condition of Bummer, posted on the bulletin board, was awaited anxiously. Finally, on November 5, came the final announcement.

"The ancient Bummer's death was posted on the canine bulletin board some days since, but we hesitated to accept the mournful tidings as correct on such doubtful authority. Later and more reliable information confirms the report, however, and we tearfully give place to the following elegy:

"He who was faithful to the end,
The noble Bummer sleeps;
Gone hence to join his better friend,
Where doggy never weeps.

"All tears are wiped from Bummer's eyes,
Good angels give him place,
E'en at the gates of Paradise,
Barking glad notes of grace.

"When Lazarus was ill, in need,
'Twas Bummer bro't him bread;
Then, brethren all, I pray take heed,
To gain such praise when dead.

"Ben Adhem's angel in his log
Writes first who love their fellow-men;
Be careful he don't place a dog
Where he should place you with his pen."

For days, lamentation in prose and verse filled the columns of the daily papers. In the columns of the *Enterprise,* Mark Twain raised his voice with the rest.

"The old vagrant, Bummer, is really dead at last, and although he was always more respected than his obsequious vassal, the dog Lazarus, his exit has not made half as much stir in the newspaper world as signalized the departure of the latter. I think it is because he died a natural death, died with friends around him to smooth his pillow and wipe the death damps from his brow and receive his last words of love and resignation; because he died full of years and honor and disease and fleas. He was permitted to die a natural death, as I have said, but poor Lazarus dies with his 'boots on,' which is to say he lost his life by violence; he gave up the ghost mysteriously, at dead of night, with none to cheer his last moments or soothe his dying pains. So the murdered dog was canonized in the newspapers, his shortcomings excused and his virtues heralded to the world; but his superior, parting with his life in the fullness of time and in due course of nature, sinks as quietly as might the mangiest cur among us. Well, let him go. In earlier days he was courted and caressed, but latterly he had lost his comeliness, his dignity had given place to a want of self-respect, which allowed him to practice mean deceptions to regain for a moment that sympathy and notice which had become necessary to his very existence, and it was evident to all that the dog had had his day. In fact, Bummer should have died sooner; there was a time when his death would have left a legacy of fame to his name; now, however, he will be forgotten in a few days. Bummer's skin is to be stuffed and placed with that of Lazarus."

Here, at least, Mark Twain proved himself a false prophet. Bummer's light shines more radiantly with the years. The skins of both dogs, to be seen at the Golden Gate Park museum, are almost fallen to pieces.

# 6

# Ed Jump

OF ED JUMP there is little to be told. He came to San Francisco—whence is not known—sometime between 1860 and 1865. He was the first portrait artist in the city, and in his time the only one. It was the period of the silhouette, the daguerreotype, and the ambrotype; the photograph came later. The daguerreotyper trundled his little cart along the boardwalks of San Francisco and took likenesses wherever he found a subject. Now, landscape artists were to be had, but no portrait artist. The pioneer ambitious to have a painting of himself sent the little daguerreotypes to China to serve as models for reproduction in oils; and hence it is that surviving oil paintings of the pioneers bear for the most part the stamp of Chinese artists.

Jump, then, as can readily be seen, was hailed for his unique genius and promptly made the idol of the town. He drew directly from life, and his subjects were the lowly as well as those in high places.

The following story of Jump comes to me from Johnny, the little ex-barber, who had it from W. Simpson Smith of Fresno, onetime boyhood friend of Johnny in the golden days of Montgomery Street, and one among the many worshipful admirers of Jump.

"A cartoon by him, even with comic attitude and exaggerated features, was so expressive of a living likeness that recognition was immediate to the eye. There is a story told of Jump and a partner, Fletcher, who in early days tramped about the mining camps of California. They arrived at one of the camps with little money, a limited stock of paint, a few tools, and a chunk of chalk. Just in front of the hotel, suspended from the limb of a tree, swung a sign on which, poorly depicted and much weatherworn, was what some bungler had intended for a bear. Jump and his partner got the job of painting a new bear. Looking over their stock, they discovered that their supply of oil colors was insufficient. None was to be had at the store, so they pieced out with water colors.

"Before commencing, Jump, in a careless, casual tone, asked the landlord, 'Want this bear fast or loose?'

" 'Why, loose, of course,' said the landlord. 'I don't want no chained bear.'

" 'All right,' said Jump, 'we'll make him loose.'

"The work was soon done, a lifelike work of art upon which an admiring multitude gazed with approving eyes. The artists received their money and after staying overnight went their way. A couple of nights afterward it rained. The rain came down in a deluge. When morning came, that splendid grizzly monarch had become the mangiest-looking bear ever seen in the Sierra. The oil colors of the background withstood the storm, but, alas, water colors were not made to outlast rainstorms.

"Some time afterward, the landlord met the artist pair and upbraided them for the unfair job they had done, saying that the bear was almost off the signboard. But Jump retorted: 'You wanted that bear loose, and it's not our fault if he leaves, is it?' "

I dislike very much to spoil so perfectly fine a story, but my good friend Ronchi of the Italian daily paper *L'Italia* tells me that this is a classic from the twelfth or thirteenth century, told of two Italian artists, Buffalimacco and Galandrino, who went about the country together painting in water colors *burle,* which is plural for *burla,* Italian for "joke." The Italian classic, however, gives the animal as a lion instead of a bear, and a cage in place of the chain.

Jump went as he came, whither no one knows. The adoration in which he was held and the regret for his departure, as well as the mystery of his disappearance, are suggested by a cartoon showing him sailing away in a balloon.

# 7

# Fire! Fire!

JOHNNY, in his youth, was a worshiper of the Volunteer Fire Department. He was by no means alone in his devotion; it was characteristic of the period. The volunteer fireman was held in like public esteem with the soldier of his country. Enlistment was an honor. No social affair of any consequence left out the Fire Department; there was no parade worthy the name which did not line up the firemen, no political election which did not reckon them as a formidable factor. The Fire Department elected the Board of Councilmen; also, its own chief and his assistants. These were paid by the city; the stewards, one to each company, were paid out of the pockets of the men. The men themselves were paid in glory. The city put up funds for the engine houses; but the men usually contributed in part, as the city money was not adequate. Out of their own pockets the men furnished their engine houses, paid for their uniforms, paid for their "blowouts" and receptions, paid their dues—and paid for their engines.

The engines were drawn by hand. The only level street was Washington. They ran, pulling their engines behind them, up hill and down, over rough cobbled streets and rough board sidewalks, in the pouring rain, and in the wind, which drove cyclones of sand before it. At night the main streets were dimly lit and the bypaths were in darkness. As the men plunged along, they were guided only by the flickering light of torches borne aloft by young boys, who flew ahead of the engines. The torches lined the walls of the engine houses like billiard cues in a poolroom. At the tap of the bell the boy snatched his torch, and away he ran to warn against holes which might prove pitfalls, and to keep a sharp lookout for nails in the board sidewalks.

The torch boys attached themselves each to his favorite engine house, but when there was a fire they observed strict neutrality. Thus Charles Robinson, dean of California artists, tells how he attached himself as torch boy to Big Six, the "Monumentals," who were for the most part Baltimoreans. If no torches were to be had in that engine house, he would run for the St. Francis Hook and Ladder, Germans; or for Lafayette Hose, the Frenchies.

How vital the torch boy was to the Fire Department this incident, related by Charles Robinson, will show:

"There was a fire one night at North Beach. Three of us were running with the engines. The first boy darted ahead, and suddenly we saw his light disappear. I was next. Down I went into a hole on top of the first boy. When the men with the engine saw two lights disappear, they knew something must have happened. So the third boy steered off in another direction. A big hole had been dug that day right in the middle of the street."

The men were also unprotected against smoke and the drenching rain from their own nozzles. Their only protection was the helmet. Three men, in eight-hour watches, stood day and night upon the tower of the City Hall looking down upon the city, laid out into eight fire districts. Where flames leaped upward, they guessed at the district. Clank! the big lever sounded upon the bell. Away went the men. They cared not for clothes; they went in hundred and twenty-five dollar suits and twenty-five dollar boots.

"The two bosses in the shop where I learned my trade," said Johnny, "belonged to the Fire Department. An alarm was struck off at the busiest time. Men were in the chairs half shaved. The bosses threw down their razors and ran out to help at the fire. And that was not in one barber shop that day, but in ten throughout the city.

"In a restaurant the boss and the waiter belonged to the Fire Department. When the fire bell struck, the waiter threw down his tray just as he was waiting on a customer, and ran out with the boss to help at the fire. And that was not in one restaurant, but all over the city."

Johnny Carroll, one of the early volunteer firemen, tells me this of Charlie Schultz, foreman of St. Francis Hook and Ladder. Schultz came to the United States in '56, sailing before the mast as a common seaman. He was a violinist and had studied under a famous master in Germany. In

San Francisco he became the leader of an orchestra, and was also the composer of many popular songs and instrumental pieces, among them the "Fireman's March," which was played at all celebrations. Schultz had a passion for going to fires and became a volunteer fireman. He carried, as a watch charm, a small golden helmet. When he led the orchestra in the "Fireman's March," he first put on his real helmet, which he always kept within reach, together with the rest of his fire-fighting paraphernalia. It is said that when Charlie Schultz played this march you could see the flames bursting from the building, you could hear the ring of the bell, you could feel the danger of the men scaling the ladders in the midst of smoke and fire and water and falling timbers, you could hear the roar of the crowd as they descended to the ground victorious. And as he played, standing there in his fire helmet, the audience beat time, the ladies tapping softly with the toes of their slippers, the men with the high heels of their boots.

At the clang of the bell, he recked little of what was happening behind the footlights. A couple of raps on the big board, a fling of his baton to the first violin, a snatch at his fire togs, and away he dashed for the door, with men and women cheering him as he rushed by.

There was that memorable evening when the great Edwin Forrest was holding the boards of the California Theater, where Schultz was leading the orchestra—you may know this was no mean event, for Johnny tells me that on one occasion when Forrest came to town, Tiffany the hatter, who had his shop on Washington Street where the Hall of Justice stands, paid a thousand dollars for two tickets for himself and his wife—well, this night, at the climax of the plot, when Forrest was holding his audience spellbound, clang! clang! rang the fire bell. Charlie Schultz was up and gone in an instant; for him, the play was "the thing" no more.

And this, Johnny Carroll tells me of himself—how he failed to get married on a spring day in '64. He was arrayed in a hundred-dollar wedding suit and had just come from having his hair dressed by Johnny; never had "Curly Jack" been so handsome or so happy. It was a Sunday, the air was like wine, his young blood sang in his veins. He stepped out gayly, his heels rapping smartly on the rough board sidewalks. He stopped at the engine house to discuss the final arrangements with his foreman, who was to be his best man. As they were talking, the fire bell rang. He tallied the count; it was his district. He looked at his watch; he had still two hours before the wedding. *Late in the afternoon,* dirty, drenched, and exhausted, he stumbled back to the engine house. He braced himself with a couple of swigs of whiskey, sank into a chair for a moment's rest—and fell asleep. *On Monday* he awoke, and, much disconcerted, hastened to the house of his prospective bride. The heart that had been so tender but the day before was adamant now against a man who, between a fire and his own wedding, could choose in favor of the fire. Ten years later he married; but the bride was another girl.

And this, Curly Jack related of the great art of Johnny, who, in the days before Kearny Street was widened, dressed the hair of everyone of note in his Washington Street shop opposite the Bank Exchange. The occasion was a great ball to be given by "High-toned Twelve." Society was always deeply stirred over any affair promoted by High-toned Twelve, and this ball promised to surpass any previous event. Curly Jack sped, after work, to have his hair dressed by Johnny. Johnny had had a busy day, shaving and curling and puffing hair—an exacting day, for each man wished to outshine the others. Often, too, Johnny had little material to work with. But here was an opportunity to display his finest art. His deft fingers fondled lovingly the thick locks of Curly Jack's head. Now, Miss Menken, the actress, had set the style in spit curls for both women and men. So, right in the mathematical middle of Curly Jack's forehead, Johnny, with much labor and love, fashioned in spit curls of beautiful lettering Curly Jack's initials, "J.C.C." They were easily the sensation of the ball.

# 8

# Independent One

INDEPENDENT 1, Empire 1, Broderick 1—so it was variously known, for it was celebrated under several names. The men were, for the most part, from New York, and boasted a target company after the then prevailing fashion among the New York firemen: hence the name "Empire." Later the company was named Broderick Engine Company, No. 1, in honor of its first foreman, the ill-fated Broderick. (I am told that Broderick was as fine a shot as Terry, but that in the fatal duel he "lost his head," just as he had in a duel fought some time before, in Oakland, in which his life was only spared because the bullet struck his watch and glanced off.)

Independent 1—and there is no doubt that this company was one of the three or four original volunteer companies—organized immediately after the "first great fire" in San Francisco, on December 24th, 1849.

Before that fire, the community had felt no need of a fire department. Before the Gold Rush, San Francisco was little more than a hamlet of fifty houses or so in the cove of Yerba Buena, with nothing near but the Mission, half church, half fortress, miles away over the sand hills, and the Presidio, still less accessible, out by the Golden Gate.

By 1849, however, the little hamlet had grown to a city, with a large population congested in a narrow area and housed in the flimsiest of structures. When fire broke out on the day before Christmas, 1849, only two engines were available to meet the emergency. One belonged to an English importing house, and was out of repair and much worn from its service in the Sandwich Islands. The other belonged to William Free, afterward foreman of No. 10; it was almost a toy machine; it had been made for President Martin Van Buren, to be used in irrigating his estates in New York City, and had been brought out by Mr. Free to be used for pumping water out of the mines. Neither engine was of much use for fighting flames. The most effective attack upon this first great fire was made by blowing up buildings with gunpowder, and by plastering the houses adjacent to the fire with mud from the streets, which in those days afforded an unlimited supply.

The loss in this fire was estimated at more than a million dollars. The most valuable property destroyed was Dennison's Exchange and the Parker House, where, after its rehabilitation, Duncan Nicol served under the proprietor, Sam Hall.

After the disaster, a mass meeting was called, at which many men were present who had served as firemen in other cities. Among them was David C. Broderick, who had served in the volunteer fire department of New York City. Not a single man who attended that first meeting is alive today. Of the surviving members of the Volunteer Department, no two agree on the story of this first organization. Some state that the Van Buren engine was the nucleus of the first fire department. Others with equal positiveness declare that no company was formed until Mayor John W. Geary, who had bought two New York side-stroke engines sent out on speculation, gave one of them to Empire No. 1 and the other to Protection No. 2. At all events, it is undisputed that after the "sixth great fire" the engine companies Empire No. 1, Protection No. 2, Howard No. 3, and Monumental No. 6 composed the solid foundation upon which was erected the powerful Volunteer Fire Department, the pride of the entire city and the love of Johnny's heart.

Dave Scannell, from foreman of Empire No. 1, rose rapidly to the rank of Chief, and held the office until the Volunteers were put out of commission by the creation of a paid department. Scannell was a brave sight at any time, but especially so in the great parades, when he appeared in his chief's white helmet, with its silver and gold lettering, his long, white coat with its two large side pockets, and carrying his silver trumpet through which to megaphone his orders.

He was tall, straight, and compact of frame, "with solid, powerful arms, and legs like a horse," according to Charles Robinson. "His head rose large and full in the back like

General Grant's, showing great bravery and determination. He was lacking, though, in the great thought processes of the General, as indicated in the lessened prominence of the forehead. And now I will tell you something of Scannell that I have never known of any other human being in the world. The first thing on coming down in the morning, he would take a dinner goblet half absinthe and half whiskey. I have seen him do that time and again at the Commercial bar. How much is a dinner goblet? Just measure one out and see."

Scannell was a great gourmet as well. He was one of the group at the famous round table in the Occidental restaurant, which was on the ground floor in the building still to be seen across from the Bank Exchange, on Washington Street, right next to Jones Alley.

In this group of Volunteers was Judge John W. Dwinelle, large and powerful of frame, weighing two hundred and fifty pounds and more, and, according to all accounts, possessed of a tremendous paunch; William Patterson, of the firm of Patterson, Wallace, & Stow, with a weight equal to that of Judge Dwinelle, and a paunch running a close second; Sam Hall, of the Parker House, a large, heavy-set man, with large head and shoulders; Alexander Campbell, who was the least in weight, and who wore little side whiskers, English fashion, in sharp contrast to the unusually heavy mustache of Judge Dwinelle; John Felton, a great civil lawyer, who is said to have been the only one of the sextette who suffered any ill effects from the too generous diet—he suffered from gout. When the season permitted, Felton had each noon at the Bank Exchange his three dozen oysters with a full quart bottle of champagne.

A table was set apart and held sacred to these six. People came just to see them eat. They went to their dinner at four or five in the afternoon and did not arise until nine or ten in the evening, when, according to Duncan, "they might have a few little drinks before retiring, which was usually quite early." On a holiday, or when Court did not convene, they sat down for breakfast at ten in the morning, often not to arise until three or four in the afternoon.

Dave Scannell and Sam Hall were the caterers. In the morning they made their regular rounds of the Washington Street markets, which ran through to Merchant Street where the fish markets are today. They went about picking up the choicest meats and tidbits for the day's dinner: the choicest cuts of beef, cocks' combs—a luxury to be had at six bits for a big mess,—sweetbreads, and shad, which sold for five dollars each though only the size of small smelts. Shad had just been planted and it was against the law to sell them; but nothing could prevent their getting into the nets. The fishermen would conceal them under their counters and await the coming of Scannell and Hall. Canvasback ducks were to be had at fifty cents a brace from the hunters, who sold them in the streets.

Chris Buckley and Sam Newman, of "Proud Ten," relate today, not without a broad smile, the great sight it was to see these men, with their fat, rosy cheeks, a genial expression on their countenances, eating canvasback duck while the blood dripped down on the napkins tucked under their chins. The ducks were cooked just thirteen minutes to the scratch, and with them was served a mighty punch, all mixed together in a great bowl—one quart each of the finest white wine and red wine, one quart each of sparkling burgundy and champagne, and a quart of the finest cognac.

If Dave Scannell was a mighty gourmet, he was yet a mightier fire fighter. He came to the Pacific Coast with Stevenson's regiment in March, 1847. He was a man without fear. His was not the style to say, "Go in there, boys"; it was, "Come on, boys." It is said that at the time of his death he had not a bone in his body that hadn't been fractured, at some time or other, in his many fierce encounters with fires and men.

# 9

# Fearless Two

THE BANK EXCHANGE, the Parker House, and the Capitol, in Platt's Hall, all might boast, after a fire alarm or a "working fire," about the "line-up" of the "high-toned" firemen; and the Occidental restaurant might pride itself on Dave Scannell, the fire chief; but to Johnny no place at such times quite equaled the Clipper. For here the "line-up" ran as high as six or seven companies, "all in their helmets," as Johnny tells, "for a cup of coffee and a big muffin." Here would assemble such foremen as Con Mooney, Sam Newman, Charlie McCann, Bob Cushing, and O'Brien, of Flood & O'Brien—who, according to Johnny, were "every bit as good firemen as Scannell, every one of them. The papers puffed Scannell up."

The Clipper restaurant was on Washington Street, on the same side as the Occidental, a block below, and just opposite Flood & O'Brien's saloon. It ran through to Jackson Street and was undisturbed by the fire of 1906. The patrons were served from a little railway which ran the entire length of the room and carried the food in dishes from the kitchen to the tables. It was a "three for two bits" house—three dishes for a quarter. The portions served were large and generous, Bordeaux fashion. It was especially famed for its coffee, to be had—twenty-five cents the price, with a ten-cent rate to firemen—together with a big muffin, or doughnuts, or a French roll ten inches long by several inches thick. People came from all about to see the waiters pour the coffee. They went about among the tables carrying two huge tin pots with long wooden handles, one pot in each hand, the one containing coffee and the other hot milk. They poured from both pots simultaneously, with an upward swish of the spouts in the air, an exact level cup of the proper proportion of milk and coffee.

Of all the firemen there assembled, to Johnny none was the equal of Con Mooney. "He was the coolest and best fireman in the city," said Johnny. "He was that cool-headed that he would never let his men go into a place without himself going in ahead to see if there was any danger.

"He was that nice and quiet-appearing a man when sitting in a chair that you never would have thought he was so game," said Barney Farley, who still lives, as of old, out near Ingleside. Barney Farley was the lifelong friend of John L. Sullivan. It was at Barney's quarters in Ingleside that Jack Dempsey the Nonpareil trained, and Jack McAuliffe, and here Farley taught Joe McAuliffe all he knew for his fight with Peter Jackson.

"But it didn't do to irritate Con Mooney," said Barney Farley. "Oh, no, no, no, no! He feared nobody and nothing. He was in Virginia City, where he ran a saloon and a billiard parlor with Joe Colburn, then the American heavyweight champion. Colburn was cutting a dash and visiting the cash drawer too frequently—till Con Mooney thought it was time for him to quit. Con took him aside and told him exactly what he thought. And Colburn after that did exactly as Con Mooney said."

"At the trial of young Kalloch for the shooting of Charles de Young," said Duncan Nicol, "all the lawyers were afraid of Con Mooney, who was called as a witness to tell how many shots had been fired. The lawyers started in to befuddle his testimony—you know how lawyers will do with a witness. But they soon found that it didn't do to meddle with Con Mooney."

"I know another thing," said Johnny. "Con Mooney fought a duel in the saloon. The two stood out on the floor to fight. They didn't have any seconds. The other man shot Con Mooney in the third finger. Con Mooney said, 'Now it's my turn to shoot.' Then he threw his pistol to the floor. I said to him, 'Why didn't you shoot?' Con Mooney was a crack shot and he had the man's life in his hands. 'Oh, pshaw!' said Con Mooney, 'I didn't want his life.'

"I'll tell you another thing," Johnny continued. "When Tim McCarthy, the prize fighter, came here from the East, he challenged Con Mooney to a fight. Con said, 'All right, if you give me time till I get this finger amputated, I'll fight you.' It was the stump of the third finger which was shot off in the duel. If he'd a-gone to fight with that stump it would have got in the way at every blow. At that, Tim McCarthy wouldn't take him up."

In a period when physical courage was reckoned supreme among the virtues, to have had that reputation for fearlessness was no mean distinction. As Barney Farley said of the prize ring, "At that time death was preferable to dishonor. Fighting was not then the physical culture exhibition it is now. Men fought with bare knuckles, London prize-ring rules, and to a finish. With their eyes all swollen, their faces battered, groggy in the legs, they would stagger up, prying their swollen eyes apart to see a bit of their opponent and crying to their seconds, 'Nurse me, nurse me along and I'll beat him yet.' "

Even as late as when John L. Sullivan, "a young man all bone and sinew, with a neck like a deer," went from village to village challenging all comers, "Lay Down" Robinson, for his cowardice in the ring, had to quit the country like a defaulter and hide for the rest of his life in Central America. Robinson was a teacher of athletics in the Olympic Club and had said he could whip Sullivan. When put to the test, he earned his sobriquet of "Lay Down," and everlasting shame, by cowering in terror to the floor.

Con Mooney, it was said, was the only man in the entire Fire Department whom Scannell feared as a rival. Owing to this professional jealousy, there was always a hitch between the two men. Con Mooney was out at the elections, always ready to be fire chief. He rose, however, no higher than assistant engineer—an office which carried a certain amount of authority then, as did that of foreman.

Mooney owned the Pony Express saloon, at Commercial and Clay streets—later at Washington and Kearny—and in conjunction with it he ran a cock and dog pit. He was often stakeholder, with a reputation for rectitude in money matters which equaled his reputation for physical fearlessness. It is said that he never owed a bill in his life and that his I O U was good in any place in the city.

"It was legal in those days to conduct cock and dog fights. It was not an uncommon thing," said Barney Farley, "to see a notice nailed on the walls of the City Hall offering a twenty-five hundred dollar purse for the best dog or cock to win. Sometimes, when I'm sitting here, I think over those days when you could nail an offer for a dog fight on the City Hall." Barney's eyes softened. "And I wonder, and smile to myself as I think, if a notice was posted like that today, how many detectives would be right on the trail to find out who put it there. It was a felony, though, to conduct prize fights. Men fought on barges, or went across to Marin County, to Sonoma, or to San Mateo. And it was an easy matter to make friends with the police. There weren't so many of 'em then as there are now."

Whether it was because Con Mooney had a competitor in Clark, next door, at Kearny and Washington, or whether it was just sportsmanship, at any rate, in the vernacular, "Con Mooney was always looking for some one to lick

Tommy Chandler," and Chandler tended bar for Clark, who was also his backer in the ring. Chandler had been a sailor. Like "Shanghai" Brown, he was a "ship's commissioner," which meant that he picked up men from the sailors' boarding houses and delivered them successfully aboard the deep-sea ships. His great record in the ring was his defeat of Billy Dwyer in a nineteen-round bout lasting twenty-three minutes, and his triumph over Dooney Harris, the English fighter, in thirty-five rounds.

As a fighter he was "licked" eventually by himself. He had had a quarrel on the water front and had returned to his quarters uptown for his pistol. Concealing the butt up his sleeve, and with the muzzle resting in his palm, covered by his fingers, he started to return to the water front for a little shooting. Suddenly, as he reached for the door, the pistol exploded in his hand. That finished Chandler for the ring, and deprived Con Mooney, once and for all, of his favorite pastime of "picking a fighter to lick Tommy Chandler."

Con Mooney met his Waterloo in little Billy Mulligan's last spree. Mulligan was a sport and politician. He was keeper of the jail under Scannell as sheriff, and, together with Scannell, was threatened with hanging by the Vigilantes for refusing to deliver Casey and Cora. Mulligan, according to Johnny, had the title of colonel, won for bravery in the War with Mexico. According to Barney Farley, he was of the same fearless mold as Con Mooney. In a quarrel in a billiard room with John Morrissey, then heavyweight champion of the world, who weighed over 200 pounds, Billy Mulligan, who weighed only 118, went for the champion and "gave Morrissey quite a run about the billiard tables."

The night of Billy Mulligan's last spree, Johnny tells me, Mulligan was throwing money around Engine Ten, and around Kearny Street. Chris Buckley, on duty at the time, tells me that at half-past one in the morning Con Mooney, Jack McNabb, and one or two other friends brought Mulligan in, on the verge of delirium tremens, for a dose of valerian to steady his nerves. Mulligan vigorously resisted all their efforts, and the next thing they knew he had given them the slip. On his way home Mulligan stopped at a pawnbroker's shop and bought a gun, and then went to his room at the St. Francis Hotel and barricaded himself in.

On the afternoon of that day, Johnny Hart, of Eureka Hose, was passing the St. Francis on his way to return a trumpet he had borrowed from a neighboring engine house. Mulligan, by that time a maniac from drink, espied him and fired one shot, and Johnny Hart fell dead on the sidewalk.

People swarmed from all directions. Mulligan, secure behind his barricade, now began to send a rain of shots to the street. Jack McNabb tried to come to the rescue. Filling a glass with valerian, he started up the stairs, calling coaxingly to Mulligan to open the door; but he wasn't more than halfway up when Mulligan shot him twice through the body. Thereupon Con Mooney bounded up, past the body of McNabb. The wholesome regard in which Con Mooney was held by all penetrated even the sodden brain of Mulligan. He sobered just an instant to call out a warning, "Con, if you come another step I'll shoot you." And Con Mooney backed down to the street.

An alarm was struck, and the police were called out. They surrounded the hotel, and stationed themselves with rifles, ready to fire, in the second-story rooms of the houses opposite. On a line strung across the street even with the second story of the hotel, a dummy man of gunny-sack and straw was swung in front of the window of Mulligan's room. His attention was drawn to the window; instantly a shot rang out—fired by Police Officer Hopkins, they say—and Mulligan fell back, dead.

# 10

# Social Three

THE HOWARD ENGINE COMPANY was best known as "Social Three." It occupied handsome quarters, unequaled perhaps by any other. It had reception rooms fitted up lavishly and elegantly, surpassed only by those of Monumental Six and High-toned Twelve, and in social affairs it was in a class by itself. Its gala nights were those given over to dances and receptions to the ladies. The fire apparatus was moved into the street to give the dance free swing, and yet be ready to move at the clang of the bell on the City Hall tower. Neither music nor dance, however seductive, could cause the men to forget even for a moment the motto emblazoned on the walls of their meeting room, "Our aim, the public good; the enemy we conquer."

Social Three had as fine a lot of fire fighters as any company in the city. Frank E. R. Whitney, its foreman, rose to the rank of second chief engineer and was the first chief elected by the paid Fire Department. Social Three had its fist and gun fighters as well, and took an active part in the final fight which resulted in legislation that put the Volunteers out of existence. It joined forces that Sunday afternoon with Monumental Six against Knickerbocker Five.

As the name implies, Knickerbocker Five was composed principally of New Yorkers, who laid the flattering unction to their souls that little old New York was the one place on earth, beyond which was nothing else. Any man who became a member of Knickerbocker Five without subscribing unconditionally to this sentiment was like a cat in a strange garret. Social Three, composed of Bostonians, had something to say of Boston as the "hub of the universe." The feeling between these two companies was thus at all times somewhat strained. But the sentiment of Monumental Six toward Knickerbocker Five went far beyond words, for Monumental Six was composed of Southerners—Baltimoreans—Secessionists; Knickerbocker Five, of Unionists.

Social Three's power was best celebrated not in exploits as gun fighters, or fist fighters, or fire fighters, but as booze fighters. In the Pacific Warehouse fire on Front Street, it is said, Social Three didn't even wait to draw the corks; just knocked the tops off the bottles of champagne.

The Pacific Warehouse belonged to the Stanford brothers; everything could be had there from a set of carpenter's tools to a bottle of whiskey or cologne. At the time of the fire there were 3000 to 5000 cases of coal oil in the warehouse, and the oil ran in a stream from Battery Street to the Bay. Every company was called out, and all responded except

No. 13. (This no doubt is a libel of the same sort as the jibe that No. 13 "had grass growing under its wheels.") The fire smoldered for a year before it was finally put out.

Following a "drunk" more glorious and protracted than usual, Social Three founded the first temperance organization in San Francisco, the Dashaway Society. Frank Whitney, the foreman, called his men together and suggested that they pledge themselves as a society to abstain from all intoxicants. Thereupon they withdrew the spirituous liquors still remaining in their commissary department, and, breaking the full bottles on the floor, "dashed away" the flowing contents. So the Dashaway Society got its name; and in time it became a great force in the temperance movement of its period. The fervor of the neophytes found expression in the following song, sung to the tune of "America":

Come, brothers, let us sing
Hail to the crystal spring,
  Fountain of health.
Its sparkling waters view,
Nurtured with holy dew,
Source of life ever new,
  Nature's true health.

Pure may our spirit be,
As the wild currents, free,
  Happy and gay.
With manly self-control
We'll *dash away* the bowl,
That would ensnare the soul
  To wine's dark sway.

Great was the display of Social Three in the parades. Each company tried to outshine all the others. They decorated their engines with a lavish hand; they polished and they furbished them. But nothing quite outshone Social Three, drawing slowly and proudly its engine of silver, shimmering in the sun—all silver-plated, except for the wheels and tires, and costing $20,000. Its foreman carried a gold trumpet, outshining even the chief's silver one. The gold trumpet was a gift made to the company at the time of its organization by one of its own members, Samuel Brannan, who thus became the company's first benefactor.

Out of appreciation for the gift of the trumpet, a movement was set on foot to change the company's name from Howard No. 3 to Brannan No. 3. To have an engine company named in one's honor was no mean distinction. In those days men climbed into society, into politics, into business, by way of the Fire Department.

Howard Engine Company had been organized in 1850 by firemen from Boston. A few days after its organization, a fine Hunneman engine, ordered early in 1849 by W. D. M. Howard on his private account, arrived from Boston by way of the Horn in the ship "Windsor Fay." Mr. Howard gave this engine to the new company. In gratitude for this assistance when aid was needed most, the men had voted unanimously that the name of the company should be that of the donor.

A strong faction in Social Three, however, remained loyal to its first benefactor, Brannan. The fight between the two factions was long drawn out. Finally the Brannan faction, stealthily, in the night, drew the shimmering engine from its shelter and ran it silently into the Bay. Days were spent in reclaiming it from the waters, and many more days in refurbishing it so that it shone again in all its pristine splendor. And there was no more talk about a change of name.

W. D. M. Howard also brought, by way of the Horn, the first complete houses from the East—fifty frame houses all "mustered in sections and fitted in Boston." Three of these were erected on Mission Street at Third, where Howard lived in one and Sam Brannan in another. It was in this wooden house of Brannan's that the first placer gold was exhibited in San Francisco.

Brannan was San Francisco's first millionaire. Barring only Harry Meiggs, none equaled him in his genius as a promoter. Nothing was beyond the range of his versatility. He promoted a Mormon colony, a trading post, a bank, and a newspaper, the *California Star,* which later was amalgamated with the *Alta California.* He promoted a theater (to keep the youth of the town from the gaming halls), a public school, a furniture factory, a summer resort, a biscuit factory, a lumber mill. He held nearly every civil office of prominence except that of mayor. He was a member of the town council, chairman of the first Vigilance Committee, and a zealously active member of the second Committee; he seemed always to be thirsty for someone's blood. And he loved display. Nothing delighted him quite so much as to wear a plug hat and harangue the multitude. He wore whiskers and dressed richly, even elegantly. As evidence that Brannan was a great local character, a vender of pies used to cry his wares at the corner of Sacramento and Montgomery, "Mince pies, apple pies, cheese pies. Everybody buys 'em. *Sam Brannan* buys 'em!"

Sam Brannan was a printer by trade. He came at the head of a Mormon colony of some two hundred and fifty men, women, and children, bringing with him a press, type, and compositors. It is said his ambition was to make California the center of Mormon power in this country. He endeavored to stimulate California's growth by glowing descriptions of the advantages to be derived from the soil and climate. He agreed to deliver to Independence, Missouri, by April, 1848, by fast express, within sixty days, two thousand copies of his newspaper setting forth the advantages of California, with two thousand more copies to follow in another sixty days. By the time of the promised second edition, the paper had to suspend operations for lack of hands to man the press—everybody had gone to the "diggin's," and the trading post which Brannan had established at Sutter's Fort under the name of C. C. Smith & Co., the first mercantile house in the Sacramento Valley, was doing a business of $150,000 a month.

Report said that Brannan got his start out of the tithes handed in to him by his Mormon brethren. He was tried by the first jury ever impaneled in San Francisco, and was acquitted. The gossip of the day, however, was this: Brannan made out a set of books perfectly correct in every particular with items such as: "Loaned to the Lord, John Smith, $100.00; loaned to the Lord, Robert Brown, $150.00," and so on. In response to protests against further payment of tithes to Brannan, Brigham Young sent emissaries to shear Brannan of his power and take over the accounts. Brannan received them with the utmost cordiality. He showed them his books with their swelling accounts. They requested, in the name of Brigham Young, that he turn the books and the cash over to them. "What has Brigham Young to do with it?" blandly inquired Brannan. "This is loaned to the Lord, and when the Lord wishes it He can come down and get it."

Brannan was a man of many contradictions and strong impulses. As nothing was beyond the grasp of his money-getting, so, equally, nothing was beyond the range of his money-giving—saloons, churches, widows, cemeteries. He gave to the Odd Fellows, for the burial of their dead, property valued in 1916 at half a million. A widow, the proprietress of a fashionable boarding house, who later married all her daughters advantageously to men of note, was in distress and applied to Brannan. He agreed to give her a monthly stipend of one hundred dollars, and for a while she went in person to get it. One month she sent her maid. "Where is your mistress?" asked Brannan. "She was busy this morning and couldn't come," said the maid. "Then," said Brannan, "she can't be in much need of money." And not another cent did she ever receive.

When on his periodic sprees, Brannan invited the whole town. At those times a thousand dollars a night was none too much; he threw his money away "like wheat before chickens." If he had no ready money, he wrote across the end of an envelope his name and the amount. Each barkeeper the next morning appeared at the office of Brannan's nephew, Alexander Badlam, who paid the accounts without question.

Brannan finally went broke building the Napa Valley Railroad and the summer resort of Calistoga. He assumed a heavy mortgage which he was unable to meet. Drink put on the finishing touches. He went to Mexico to try to realize on his Yaqui land grants, which the Mexican government had given him in consideration of his assistance with arms and money at the time of its trouble with the Emperor Maximilian, but had no success.

Charles Robinson relates that when Brannan returned in the early 'seventies to San Francisco, he came, one cold, rainy day into Robinson's studio. He was wet, bedraggled, and liquored up. His clothes were threadbare and his shoes torn. He wept as they talked together of the old happy days. And Johnny says that when, at this same time, Brannan paid a visit to Pioneer Hall and saw on the wall his photograph, showing him as a tall, handsome man, with large, beautiful eyes, and richly attired, the tears rolled down his cheeks.

Frank Garcia finally advanced Brannan some money on his Mexican claims, but the Yaquis would never allow him to take possession. He died in Escondido, San Diego County, in 1889, alone and in comparative poverty.

# 11

# High-toned Twelve

IT WAS IN 1855 that a new invention, the steam fire engine, made its first appearance in New York City. On all sides it was received with derision and declared impossible for practical purposes. The *Scientific American,* alone, seems to have had the temerity to declare that the "steamer would excel the hand engine." For this rash statement its editors were heaped with censure as "unscientific." To determine the much mooted question of whether the steamer or the hand engine was superior, a public trial was had this same year. The hand engine won, and this victory for the old order against the new was triumphantly heralded in the local newspapers. They opened their columns wide to fulsome praise in prose and verse of the hand engine, with equal ridicule of the steamer.

So strong was the opposition that not until 1862 was San Francisco to see a steam engine. Peter Donahue, the head of the Union Iron Works and a machinist by trade, became interested in the new invention and the possibility of using it for pumping water at the plant, and set sail for New York to investigate and perhaps to purchase one. The event created much excitement among the "boys" of the shop. They chartered a boat and gave Donahue a great send-off.

Hardly had Donahue left when High-toned Twelve had it in mind to outshine the other engine companies by being the first to purchase a steamer, and set about giving its order for one to be sent by way of the Horn. Somehow or other Big Six got wind of what was up. Hurriedly, yet as secretly and stealthily as High-toned Twelve had acted, the men of Big Six took up a collection among themselves to get a machine of their own. They dispatched an order by Pony Express, which took only ten and a half days to reach St. Joseph, Missouri, the western terminus of the railroad. The order called for a steamer—old or new, so long as it was a steamer—to be sent immediately by way of the Isthmus.

When the time drew near for the arrival of the steamer ordered by Big Six, George Hossefross, the foreman, betook himself for a little social visit over to the foreman of High-toned Twelve. In the course of conversation, Hossefross made a bet of five hundred dollars that Big Six would have a steamer in their engine house on the hill before High-toned Twelve had theirs from the hold of the ship. Twelve, wise in its own conceit, eagerly took up the bet. Big Six's steamer arrived ahead even of Peter Donahue's, and what Big Six lost in freight charges by the Isthmus route, it made up by winning the bet. High-toned Twelve never quite forgave Big Six for the trick it played them. It was this steamer, drawn by hand, a thing of joy and rejoicing to Big Six, which became a thing of mourning, the instrument of death to two of its members, Bohen and Washington, when they made a reckless dash without a brake down the Washington Street hill to the Niantic Hotel fire.

High-toned Twelve's only hope now for supremacy was to be the first to attach horses to a steamer. This idea was hailed by the other companies with derision and stigmatized as Twelve's crowning attempt to evade work.

High-toned Twelve had long been dubbed the "Featherbed Firemen" and "Patent Leather Firemen." They went to a fire, some said, in frock coats and patent leather boots, and in stovepipe hats because they disliked the regulation helmet. Furthermore, it was said that at the sight of a mud puddle, fearful of getting their feet wet, they would drop their rope and expect the engine to follow on after, and it was often asserted that if ever High-toned Twelve ran ahead in a race to a fire, it would surely be beaten at a mud puddle.

At first the man-drawn engines were well on their way to a fire before High-toned Twelve's horses had even reached the door. In two or three weeks, however, when the horses were thoroughly trained to the stroke of the bell, they left the men on foot far in the rear. High-toned Twelve had finally triumphed. Other firemen began to see that to "draw the soulcase" out of themselves doing what horses could do with ease was not so much an evidence of physical prowess as a mark of folly.

The victory of the steamer was only won through the persistence of David D. Hayes. Hayes was a machinist by trade and the inventor of the Hayes truck, which revolutionized fire-fighting methods and did away entirely with the old hand-splice ladder. He had been for years a member of the volunteer department in New York City, and brought with him to San Francisco, by way of Panama, five steam engines of the Amoskeag patent. These had been ordered by the Board of Supervisors as part of its plans for a paid fire department. But prejudice was strong against these new steamers and it seemed amply justified when old Big Betsy, also called the "Big Coffee Kettle," beat a new Amoskeag-patent engine—as the old and established have, in initial tests, the habit of doing against the new and untried.

Hayes bided his time, full of faith. He was a great favorite around Social Three. He was the honored guest at their chowderies, their glee clubs, and their balls and parties. He exacted a promise from them to give him a chance to show what his engine could do by letting him go to the next big fire, and he pledged the members to man his engine. So, when Social Three saw Hayes's opportunity in a grocery-store fire which started in the wholesale district, they flashed him the signal.

Godfrey Fisher—the only member, save one, still alive of Social Three—was the stoker. Though he knew little of stoking, he was full of the resourcefulness of the volunteer. Nor were underwriters present in those days to check the activity of the axe. Fisher's eyes lit upon packing boxes, fine fuel for his engine. Down swung the axe, splitting the boxes into suitable splinters.

"Keep her up to a hundred!" shouted Hayes. The boxes gave out. The gauge dropped, showing only seventy pounds' pressure. Again the voice of Hayes: "Keep her up to a hundred!" Fisher's eyes fell upon some fine hams. He seized one and threw it into the fire box. It made a magnificent blaze. With the zeal of the neophyte he now began piling in ham after ham. The gauge mounted to a hundred and twenty, and suddenly a shout of consternation broke in upon the hilarious stoker. "Open up, there!" shouted Hayes, in alarm. "Keep her down to a hundred!"

Fisher flung wide the valves. He never forgot this, his first and only experience at stoking. The worry and trouble in controlling the steam, now too suddenly above the mark and now too much below, is vivid in his memory today. Finally, he had the Amoskeag engine steadily humming under a hundred pounds' pressure and easily throwing four streams of water to the two thrown by the hand engine.

Hayes's became the pioneer engine, Independent No. 1, of the paid Fire Department. But the gain in efficiency proved the beginning of the end for the joyously racing volunteers.

# 12

# Fortune's Kings

DUNCAN NICOL will show it to you—the sealed door at the Bank Exchange. It is above the stairway leading to the cellar. Behind that sealed door the former proprietors of the Bank Exchange signed away to A. P. Hotaling, as you would snap your fingers, the beginning of his fortune—which by the time of his death had grown to millions.

The stairway was spiral in the old days, and led directly to the door, which opened at the rear upon a courtyard—still to be seen—and at the side upon the wholesale department of the Bank Exchange, where, together with a large stock of imported liquors, the proprietors carried a certain Eastern brand of Bourbon whiskey, very smooth.

Money flowed like water in those days. Gold was weighed on the grocer's scales. Twenty thousand dollars was often staked on the turn of a single card, twenty-dollar gold pieces on a single throw of the dice. Much of the gold flowed into the Bank Exchange, the most fashionable saloon of the day.

A drink was two bits, and only European brands were asked for. The proprietors, overwhelmed and wishing no longer to be bothered with the Eastern whiskey, turned the agency over to Hotaling, who was then doing a liquor business in a small and quiet way.

The Civil War broke out. A prohibitive tax was placed upon the imported liquors, and demand shifted to the domestic brands. Then came the boom of the Comstock. Hotaling built up a tremendous business in Virginia City as well as in San Francisco. He sold fifty-five barrels a week, on the average, to Collins & Wheeland, and the barrels stood in front of their place, it is said, "like waves on the sidewalk."

The barrels were in themselves an advertisement; they were of a peculiar shape and cooperage. Competitors bought up the empties to fill with an imitation blend. Out of the demand for this particular barrel Michael King made a fortune of $200,000.

Michael King was known as the "Barrel King." He could neither read nor write. He was ill-kempt, and the boys stoned him on the streets for a miser. He dressed in rags. He spent next to nothing for food. Drink he had for the asking, from the cellarmen. The empties which he bought at two dollars apiece, he retailed to the wholesalers at fifty apiece; to save drayage he trundled the barrels along the streets with a stick, so expertly that people stopped to watch him. He never trusted his fortune to the banks, but hid it in out-of-the-way corners. He finally went insane over a $10,000 debt he couldn't collect, and died in the Asylum.

Below the Bank Exchange, on the same side of Washington Street and next the market, was the saloon of Flood & O'Brien. Across the street was the Clipper restaurant, with the Custom House and the Post Office a little below. Flood & O'Brien's saloon, which had all the market trade, was thus in line to catch much of the excitement and gossip of the day, as well as the casual trade. It was a wholesome-looking place. The miners coming to town liked to drop in, and over the bar talk in a chummy sort of way about the mines and the strikes that had been made, and to volunteer tips on prospective stock gambles.

Flood and O'Brien were quiet, conservative men, who attended strictly to business. They made money in the saloon, and with part of it they speculated in mining stocks. They made the acquaintance of two miners, Mackay and Fair. The four worked together. They were among the first at Virginia City, where, working up gradually, they got control of the Comstock. They were to go down in the mining history of California as the "Big Four."

Flood was a rather grouchy fellow. O'Brien was a big, liberal-hearted Irishman, much given to card playing. He played, according to all accounts, mainly for the drinks, even in the days of his greatest affluence. He was fond of euchre and of the game of hearts. Of a night, before the days of the Comstock, when it was quiet in the saloon, he and Ed Stahle would play euchre in the back room.

Ed Stahle kept the fashionable baths and barber shop in the Montgomery Block. He had the baths across the way before the Montgomery Block was built; in fact, he saw it built. Stahle was a strong adherent of the Vigilantes, and was vigorously opposed to many of his patrons, especially prominent judges and lawyers who were adherents of the Law and Order side. Many were the heated arguments, almost to the danger point, that arose in bath and barber's chair. He lived on the top floor of the building with his family, and was there when James King of William was brought in to die.

After the Comstock made the saloon no longer a necessity, O'Brien could be seen almost any day in the week playing cards either at Louis Teese's place, or with Henry White, who kept a faro bank at Third and Market, and who, much like O'Brien, was a man who attended strictly to business and played only for the drinks. Or O'Brien might be seen at Phil McGovern's in a game of hearts with Jack Harold and John Mason, brewers, or with Ed Buckley, the license collector, and Colonel Bateman, the contractor. Bateman's method of constructing sewers was extremely simple; when an order for a sewer was given, he bought up empty barrels and built his line by placing them end to end.

While the Comstock was booming, mines in which Sharon and Ralston were interested, such as the Ophir and Hale and Norcross, were petering out. The rivalry between these mine owners was bitter. Ralston and Sharon made a threat that they would drive Flood and O'Brien back to selling whiskey over the counter. "If so," replied Flood and O'Brien, "we will be selling whiskey over the counter of the Bank of California." Had they wished, they could have done so. Looking toward the opening of their own bank, the Bank of Nevada, Flood and O'Brien had deposited a million dollars with the Bank of California. In a weak moment the Ralston and Sharon bank allowed them to withdraw the million—and the Bank of California failed.

Flood never belonged to the Volunteers, but O'Brien was an active fireman and foreman of California Engine, No. 4, which lay at the edge of Happy Valley, on Market Street between Sansome and Montgomery. Close to California Four, at Second and Howard, was the engine house of Tiger Fourteen, and to it belonged all of Happy Valley's grocers and butchers; it was their only social center.

California Four was composed mainly of men who worked in the Peter Donahue foundry and in the planing mills. Enrolled as a member, and at one time the foreman of this company, was Isaiah W. Lees, a machinist in the foundry, where his brother was foreman boilermaker. Isaiah was to become widely known as the city's chief of police and the greatest detective of the nation. Another member of Tiger Fourteen was Claus Spreckels, retail grocer.

Claus Spreckels had a large family trade in sugar. Housewives made much of baking cakes and pies and cookies and putting up preserves. Spreckels sold so much sugar to the family trade that he started a small refinery, a little bit of a place in a wooden building, 50 by 100 feet, at Ninth and Brannan streets. He was to become the "sugar king" of the West, and in later years a prominent financier.

Claus Spreckels paid his dues regularly to Tiger Fourteen, but he did little or no active work as a fireman. But then, Tiger Fourteen could scarcely be classed with the active companies; it was second in reputation to Engine Thirteen, which had "the grass growing under its wheels." Nor had California Four much more opportunity to display activity. The two companies were too far from the heart of town to know either great fire fighting or the intense rivalry that existed between such companies as Knickerbocker Five and Big Six, or Engines Two and Ten.

California Four and Tiger Fourteen lived amicably together except for one memorable fight, and that was a fluke. The bell sounded for a fire in Waverly Place. Tiger Fourteen's engine was being repaired, so the company ran with its hose cart only, which is easy running. California Four had a few blocks the advantage at the start, but had two sets of men to be handled, and a cart and an engine. Tiger Fourteen caught up with them on Clay Street. The two engines collided, the hubs of the wheels interlocking. Sam McDowell, on the front of Tiger Fourteen's rope, held the rival engine fast by winding the rope of his cart to a basement railing at his side. California Four demanded the release of its wheels. Tiger Fourteen flung its ultimatum—the right of way as victors in the race. California Four refused, a fight ensued, the fire was forgotten. The foreman of Tiger Fourteen with his trumpet scored a bruised head, and Sam McDowell, with his fist, a bloody nose. The police intervened, arresting the members of both companies.

On the way to the station the party met Chief Scannell.

"Release those boys," said Scannell to the officers. "I will be responsible for them." Then he turned and in a tone of reprimand said, "Boys, man your ropes and return home."

They went like naughty children.

But California Four had its future heroes. William Alvord, who lived at Folsom and Second in Happy Valley, was to be president of a bank; and William T. Coleman would go down in history as the president of the Vigilante Committee that hanged Casey and Cora and ran Ned McGowan out of town. McGowan returned, years later, broken in health, in spirits, and in pocketbook, and it was Coleman who paid for his last days in the hospital and the expenses of his burial.

James Wethered, at Big Six, was to be immortalized in the reflected glory of his wife, the daughter of Samuel Woodworth, author of "The Old Oaken Bucket." At Ten Engine was a Justice of the Peace of the Second District, one Robert Tobin, who was to be president of a bank. And at Liberty Hose was Tom Sawyer, sailor, adventurer, fire fighter, who was to be "crowned with immortality" as the inspiration of Mark Twain's *The Adventures of Tom Sawyer*. To him was dedicated this first book of America's greatest humorist.

Glory came to the firemen, fire or no.

# 13

# Songs of the Volunteers

THE MAJORITY of men in San Francisco, in the early 'fifties, had had some experience of the sea, either having shipped before the mast or sailed as passengers on the long voyage from the Isthmus or around the Horn. Engine No. 8, in fact, was composed of so many sailors that it was never known otherwise than as Sailor Eight. It was the sailors who introduced the chantey into the Fire Department, to be sung especially at the laborious task of pumping water by hand.

I give here a chantey which was sung by all the companies and was a favorite of Engine Ten and Engine Fourteen. It illustrates admirably the sailors' influence upon San Francisco; it carries, as well, the impress of the War with Mexico (many of the pioneers made directly from that war for the gold fields); and it pictures the firemen's life.

Santa Anna is dead and gone,
  Hurrah, Santa Anna!
Oh, we won our day at Monterrey,
  All on the plains of Mexico.

Oh, Mexico and Texas, too,
  Hurrah, Santa Anna!
I wouldn't be Santy's son, you know,
  All on the plains of Mexico.

Number One, she's always on the run,
  Hurrah, Santa Anna!
Number Two always had a bully crew,
  All on the plains of Mexico.

Number Three had a chowderie,
  Hurrah, Santa Anna!
Number Four is lying at the door,
  All on the plains of Mexico.

Number Five is always alive,
  Hurrah, Santa Anna!
Number Six is a bully set of bricks,
  All on the plains of Mexico.

Number Seven will never get to heaven,
  Hurrah, Santa Anna!
Number Eight is always late,
  All on the plains of Mexico.

Number Nine is never on time,
  Hurrah, Santa Anna!
Number Ten had a great set of men,
  All on the plains of Mexico.

Number Eleven was just like seven,
  Hurrah, Santa Anna!
Number Twelve is on the shelf,
  All on the plains of Mexico.

Number Thirteen was never to be seen,
  Hurrah, Santa Anna!
Number Fourteen was always a-courtin',
  All on the plains of Mexico.

A favorite of Knickerbocker Five was "Hunt the Buffalo." Till the day of his death it was the special delight of Steve Bunner, who in the days of the Volunteer Fire Department was assistant foreman of the Knickerbockers. No banquet was ever quite complete without this song. It had been brought from New York by Curly Jack Carroll, who sang it for the first time in San Francisco at the Sarsfield fire. The Sarsfield Hotel was packed to overflowing that night by refugees from floods at Sacramento. The rain descended in torrents. Above the rain, the pumping of the engines, the hoarse cries of command, the shrieks of the terror-stricken, rose the resounding bass voice of Curly Jack in "Hunt the Buffalo."

Another song of the 'fifties, beloved by all, and enchanting alike the firemen and the people, was "The Fireman's Bride." It is a key to the heart of the fireman and to the glamour which surrounded him, and a glowing account, as well, of his glory and his deeds. Curly Jack was the first man to hear it in San Francisco. He had it from Felix Desmond, who brought it down from Sacramento. It was in this manner, in the old days, that songs were disseminated on this coast; a good singer had it from some stranger, or caught it from an actor on the stage.

### THE FIREMAN'S BRIDE

As I strolled out on a fine summer's evening,
The weather it was fine and clear,
I overheard a tender mother
Conversing with her daughter dear,

Saying, "Daughter, dear, I would like you to marry,
No longer lead a single life."
"Yes, dear mother, I am going to marry,
I'm going to be a fireman's wife."

CHORUS

Who wouldn't be a fireman's darling?
Who wouldn't be a fireman's bride?
I'm going to be a fireman's lover,
I'm going to be a fireman's wife.

Firemen they are young and foolish,
Firemen they are inclined to roam,
Firemen they would leave you broken-hearted,
They would leave your heart forlorn.
Give me the lad with the red fire shirt on,
Give me my heart's delight,
Give me the lad with the fire coat and hat on,
For I'm going to be a fireman's bride.

[*Repeat chorus*]

Hark, don't you hear the Hall bell a-ringing?
Hark, don't you hear the doomful sound?
Hark, don't you hear the firemen a-running?
As they cry, "Pull on, brave boys, pull on!"
"Number One, start your water!"
"Light up!" "Pick up and play your water high!"
"Don't you see the ladder up against the building?"
Out of the crowd steps a brave fire boy.

[*Repeat chorus*]

Up, up the ladder, see how he's a-tripping,
Without dread and without fear.
Into the flames see how he's a-going,
As he cries aloud, "Brave boys, we are here!"

Down, down the ladder, see how he's a-coming,
Without dread and without fear.
In his arm he carries a mother;
See how she clings to her baby dear.

[*Repeat chorus*]

The fire's all out,
And we can work no longer.
Take up! Reel up! And play your ladders high!
Command your rope! And we'll clean her in the
 morning,
We are a bully good crew,
And if we want to try.

[*Final repetition of chorus*]

Felix Desmond was always enthusiastically received at all the engine houses. Wherever he went he had to sing, above all else, "Sally in Our Alley." A close second was Desmond's own "Midnight Bells," which, in part, celebrated defiantly the old-time volunteer.

You talk of your modern reforms,
Of the paid jacks and all of their charms
And things new-fangled and queer;
But give me the old Volunteer.
With your money you'll make a great clatter,
You'll make a great clatter,
You'll make a great clatter,
But where will you get your water?
 That is just what,
 That is just what is the matter.

 Then lift her, laddies;
 Lift her, laddies;
 Lift her, laddies, away!

Of all the engine companies Social Three had the best singers. They were looked upon, however, as "a sentimental lot of fellows," who rested beside the water hydrant between pumpings and sang "Come Where My Love Lies Dreaming"—the particular favorite of Social Three's finest singer, Joe Augustus,—"Silver Bells of Memory," "Suwanee River," "Oft in the Stilly Night," "Life on the Ocean Wave," "Rory O'Moore," "Silver Moon," and "The Low-backed Car."

Of interest, even to this day, to any and all firemen is "Our Engine on the Hill," written by Charles Rhoades, and dedicated to Monumental Six upon the tragic death of two of its members. Monumental Six was housed on the hill at Brenham Place. The Niantic Hotel at Clay and Sansome was on fire. Down Washington Street raced Monumental Six—without brakes. Washington Street was steeper then than it is now; it has since been graded. Walter Bohen, the foreman, and James H. Washington, a member, were thrown under the boiler, which "kept punching down upon them." Both were killed.

There's Bohen and Washington, too—
Brave boys as ever drew breath—
Who, when the "Hall" rang, nobly jumped for the tongue,
And went forth to battle with death!
How bravely they met their sad fate!
To save them was past human skill;
They sank, with a groan, while onward alone
Sped our Engine that's housed on the Hill.

# 14

# The Fight for the Foxtail

IT WAS FRANCIS ATKINSON, "Cockeyed Frank," steward of Ten Engine, who put up the foxtail as a trophy for the company that should win a race to a fire. He came from the Blue Grass region of Kentucky, and naturally had sporting blood in his veins.

It happened, one day, that Proud Ten—"Crescent Ten," as it was sometimes known, because most of its men came from New Orleans—passed clean ahead of another engine in a race to a fire. In their elation the men stuck a broom on top of the engine to indicate the "clean sweep." As a less unwieldy and more enduring trophy, Cockeyed Frank substituted the foxtail.

In time the foxtail grew to be an institution of the Volunteer Fire Department. An unwritten law governed its possession: the company starting with it to a fire but losing the race must go straight to the engine house of the winning company, once the fire was out, and there make formal presentation of the foxtail to the foreman and his men.

The hose boys, proudly aping their elders, put up their own foxtail, and competed for it as keenly as did the men for theirs. Johnny, the little ex-barber, belonged to the hose boys of California Four. In a fight this company had with a rival, the hose boys' foxtail came to a sad end. It was at the time of a warehouse fire at Battery and Sacramento streets. In the midst of flying fists and spanners, which incidentally broke several heads, the foxtail was rent in twain. Each company claimed its half and refused ever afterward to give it up.

For a long time—close to a year, some say—Ten Engine held undisputed right to *the* foxtail. Then, one day, Two Engine outdistanced Ten Engine, and a fierce rivalry began which ended only when Ten Engine moved up Stockton Street, too far from the center of town to be in position for keen competition with anybody.

Rivalry among the different companies was intense at all times, and at all points. For the volunteer firemen, whether in pursuit of duty or not, to fight was life. Historic is the fierce contest that Vigilant Nine and Big Six waged for supremacy in the height of the "water throw" of their engines. Charles Robinson, the artist, recalls from boyhood memory the cold, damp Thanksgiving Day of the contest, and the rivals in their struggle for supremacy. Big Six shot its stream easily above the top of the Liberty Pole in the Plaza—now Portsmouth Square. Vigilant Nine tried to equal this by every trick, even holding its stream against the pole in the hope that the impact would shoot the water upward, but in vain. In anger, the baffled hosemen turned the full force of their water on the men of Big Six, who returned in kind. The populace fled.

Later, in a contest at Sacramento, Big Six broke all records for a hand engine by a high throw of 229 feet, 8 inches. This record it paraded upon its engine, engraved on a metal plate, together with the word "Chief." Big Six boasted, too, the biggest hand engine, the first steam engine, an alarm bell second only to the bell in the City Hall tower, and the first ball given in the Department—tickets at twenty dollars and strictly full dress required.

Independent One—or Empire One, or Broderick One, as you will—boasted its crack riflemen; it had a military organization called the Empire Guards. Once a year the Empire Guards went on an excursion and in the presence of an awed throng competed for prizes in target shooting. Knickerbocker Five preened itself on having New York for a birthplace. It had also as a member one Charles McMahon, nicknamed "Charlie the Bone-breaker" because he hit so hard that every time he landed he broke a bone in his own hand. High-toned Twelve, as has been mentioned before, prided itself on its first families, and Social Three on its piano and glee club, and its silver-plated engine.

Two and Ten Engines, however, disdained these vain forms of rivalry. They held in thinly veiled contempt the members of Social Three, who decked themselves out in gold capes on parade, and of High-toned Twelve, with their plug hats and patent leather boots, and the men of other companies who flashed jewelry on their red shirts. Two and Ten prided themselves on the severe simplicity of their uniform. Others might turn for the smiles of the ladies who had come to watch a parade; Two and Ten marched looking straight ahead, with never a glance to right or left. They took joy only in that supremacy which arose from strength of muscle, quickness of perception, fleetness of foot, and matchless daring and courage. To these two companies the greatest glory of all was possession of the foxtail, symbol of the qualities that went to the making of a great fire fighter.

Possession of the foxtail marked a company as the first to get water, which was done by attaching a suction pipe to the hose and lowering it into a cistern. The pipes were of brass, or of copper-riveted leather, and were called "blunderbusses." For coupling them, the firemen carried spanners, which, with their long handles stuck in the users' belts, presented the appearance of bayonets.

To get the pipe, and to be able to hold it, meant enjoyment of the highest of battle honors—the position of first at the fire and last to leave. To hold the pipe meant, also, to get the greatest drenching. It meant being beaten over the head with spanner and blunderbuss in the fierce struggle for possession. It meant straining every muscle to retain the pipe against the terrific force of the water. Gus Finn, still with powerful shoulders at seventy, relates how the pipe once in getting away knocked him clean down the street. Yet such was the valor of the volunteers that on all sides arose the cry, "Give *me* the pipe! I'll hold her!"

Two men held the tongue of the engine, and each had the right to his side of the pipe, and also the right to award it to whomsoever he wished in his company. The rest of the men took the ropes. Every man wished to be at the tongue: the men at the tongue must be fleet of foot; they did the steering. Every man at the stroke of the bell sprang for the tongue.

Much was to be gained in getting the start. The light sleeper had the advantage over the heavy sleeper. There were no gongs, only the clang of the bell in the City Hall. The man at the head of the stairs had the advantage of the man in the rear; there were no poles for sliding down to the engine from the bunkroom. Many were the tricks played to gain an advantage. One was to place a man's boots with heels foremost instead of toes. A few seconds made a vast difference. Yet many a man at the end of the room, more alert in gathering his senses when awakened, might outstrip the man at the head of the stairs.

"Bunkers," men who slept in the engine house, were a great advantage to a company in getting first to a fire. Ten Engine had the greatest number of bunkers, thirty-nine bunking at one time in its house. It was said that Ten Engine on the way south to a fire would pass Big Six's engine house in Brenham Place as Big Six was just getting out.

Not only had Ten Engine the greatest number of bunkers, but its men were all enthusiasts, "shingle-eaters," every man of them. The shingle-eater was the man quick with the axe and the most expert in tearing shingles from a house in order to gain access to the fire. Among the most enthusiastic of Ten's shingle-eaters was a certain caulker, notorious as the laziest man in town—so lazy that he wouldn't wash, yet always first at fires. He became, in time, an assemblyman in the State legislature.

The men of Ten Engine were likewise all runners. Johnny McGreevy, the "Mountain Buck," was a member. He held the championship from Mike Gulley of Engine One, and lost it eventually to Barney Cosgrove of California Four. It was Johnny McGreevy, the Mountain Buck, who was selected by Proud Ten to hold the tongue of the engine and roll it downhill, in the great run it made on the day before the first of the annual firemen's parades. For years McGreevy was in the Police Department, side partner of Policeman Hopkins, who fired the shot that killed Billy Mulligan in the St. Francis Hotel. He is watchman, these days, in the Twin Peaks tunnel, and still lithe as a deer. He lives within a few blocks of Curly Jack Carroll, his lifelong friend. It was Curly Jack who trained him for his greatest race.

The proudest day in all the history of the old Fire Department was May 4th, 1862, the first Firemen's Day, a day officially set apart for the annual and particular glorification of the firemen of San Francisco. There had been a firemen's parade on Washington's Birthday, 1854; but the rains were heavy and the mud was deep in the streets, so that little interest was shown in the event. For various reasons—money stringency, bank failures, and the like—there was no parade of any note for some years afterward.

In 1861, the Board of Councilmen determined to have an annual parade to show the citizens the splendor and efficiency of the Department they so ardently supported. The parade, it was further determined, should take place only upon a day devoid of other significance. After much deliberation, May 4th was hit upon; it was a day when, in all probability, there would be no rain. It was likewise the anniversary of the great fire of 1851. On Bunker Hill Day, June 17th, of this year 1861 there would be an inaugural ceremony at which the official announcement of Firemen's Day would be made.

At ten o'clock on Bunker Hill Day the fire bell sounded a general alarm. The people, long accustomed to this, the dread signal of a "call to arms" by the Vigilance Committee, flocked excitedly to the streets. This time, however, the signal was for the engine companies to fling wide their doors and, with their engines festooned with flowers and ribbons and flags, to proceed along streets canopied in flags and bunting to Platt's Hall, there to start the parade.

The proudest company of all was Proud Ten. The ladies of the community had sought to honor their favorite house on this day by public tokens of esteem. Throughout the community, both men and women had linked themselves, in some manner, to some engine house, either by pulling with the regular volunteers at a fire, or through money donations, or social favoritism. Many now took part in the parade—Ten Engine was said to have the largest line-up of actors, and Manhattan Two, of supers.

Early that morning, before the parade, Big Six had received the gift of a magnificent wreath in the center of which was the figure "6." Tiger Fourteen received, as the parade was under way, a patriotic wreath; from a line stretched across the street and lowered at the right moment, the wreath was dropped directly into the hands of the foreman. Within it was a circle of Union rosettes—it was a period of bitterly opposed Union and Secession sentiment—and within the circle a gold star, while surmounting all was a golden eagle with Union flags gripped in its talons. Most fitting tribute of all, however, was the banner presented to Proud Ten in recognition of its "intrepid daring." The banner was fringed with gold bullion and the top of the pole was surmounted by a gilt crescent and festooned in blue and white silk. On the front of the banner was a painting of the new Cowing engine which the Company was expecting, and an inscription, in white silk, of the Company's motto, "Loyalty and Preservation."

And now the time was drawing near to Firemen's Day. Manhattan Two still held the foxtail. Proud Ten still wanted it, as the single and only fitting adornment for its engine; the men of Proud Ten scorned at any time to bedeck their machine with flowers and ribbons. They had, moreover, an especial pride in the foxtail as an institution originating in their own company. To see it now, at such a time, in the hands of their deadliest rival, was not to be borne.

Suspicious at all times of Ten Engine, Manhattan Two, as May 4th drew near, grew doubly suspicious. It redoubled its vigilance. It grew leary of every alarm of fire in fear of a "put-up job," or "staged fire," on the part of Ten Engine. Indeed, only through the superior wisdom of George Blasdell, the assistant foreman of Manhattan Two, was the foxtail saved from falling into the hands of the enemy.

The "staged fire" was a phenomenon that grew out of zeal for possession of the trophy. The law of the foxtail was that the company flying it must challenge all others to take it away in a race to a fire. Now a genuine fire left much to be desired as a crucial occasion. It might occur in the wrong location, uphill, or too close for a good run. Most of the fake fires were staged in the Seventh District, which was anywhere in the direction of Bush Hill or Rincon Hill and beyond. To a fire in this district the race was long and all downhill.

In staging a fire, empty shacks, or tar barrels stealthily carted out to the district, were set ablaze, and the bell ringer in the tower was "fixed." A bright blaze was necessary; otherwise the bell ringer might be "called up" and "broke"—for although the department was a volunteer one it was nevertheless under the authority of the city government. There were three bell ringers, each elected for one year by a board of delegates, two delegates from each company. Two Engine and Ten Engine, in their zeal for the foxtail, were always active in firemen's politics, each trying to engineer the appointment of one of its own men as bell ringer. The notorious ship caulker of Ten Engine was "on the bell" this year.

To hasten the progress of the plotters' engine, relays of fresh men were "planted" on the sidewalks, like innocent bystanders, all along the way. Picked men only could be used in the relays. The men with the engine, upon coming to the place where a relay was stationed, would pull up only just enough for the relay to jump under the rope, take hold, and be off on the wings of Mercury.

These fake fires were staged with so much ingenuity and so much secrecy as to deceive the wisest among the firemen. It was only because a member of Ten Engine was green and not acquainted with the personnel of the other engine companies that Two Engine was able to defeat Ten Engine's put-up job to get the foxtail away.

The fire was to be at twelve o'clock. Ten Engine had sent its men stealthily with tar barrels to the Seventh District. The ship caulker was in readiness in the City Hall tower. The word had been passed to the relays. All was in immediate readiness, when a green volunteer of Ten Engine was seen going down the street with a fire cap under his arm. Two men stopped him, and one of them said:

"Why are you packing that fire cap around?"

"We're going to have a fire," said the green volunteer, "at twelve o'clock, and we're going to beat Two Engine sure this time."

"Is that so?" laughed one of the men, who belonged to Two Engine. "Well, have a good time."

And the Two Engine man beat it down the street to tell his Company. It was too late for Blasdell, who was in command, to get men enough together to beat Ten Engine all the way to the fire. The bell indicated the Seventh District. Quick of wit, Blasdell shouted the order, "Up Jackson to Kearny!" Now, Two Engine lay at Jackson Street and Montgomery. The regular run to the Seventh District would have been down Montgomery. One of the men remonstrated. "I don't care where the fire is," shouted Blasdell. "Up Jackson Street!"

At Kearny, Blasdell halted. Ten Engine, coming down Kearny, also halted. The two engines stood side by side, both refusing to budge, and each goading the other with, "Why don't you start?" It was against the law to delay on the way to a fire, but Blasdell waited, hoping for reinforcements, and Ten Engine waited, hoping for a race. Suddenly Blasdell spied some of his own men and waved them in, and with a whoop and a yell away sped Two Engine through the crowd, leaving Ten Engine with nothing but its labor for the pains of its staged fire.

But Proud Ten didn't give up; it staged another fire. One of the men informed beforehand of this "fire" was Johnny Carroll. "When I see them engines coming side by side," he picks up the story, "I runs and jumps up on Ten Engine in the rear. I tries to push the engine along, I lifts it on my shoulder. Johnny McGreevy was on the tongue. 'Jack,' he hollers to me, 'get on the rope!' I got on the rope. We picked up fresh men along the sidewalk. We passed Two Engine getting into Market Street. As we passed, George Blasdell went faint.

"That night, Con Mooney, the foreman of Two Engine, came up with his committee to Ten Engine and turned over the foxtail.

" 'We'll get it back,' he said, 'before morning.'

"The morning would be May 4th, the day for the great parade. That night there was little sleep for any of us in Ten Engine. The foxtail was attached to a bell that jingled at the slightest touch. But we weren't taking any chances. We slept in chairs throughout the night, guarding the foxtail. So when it came time for the parade, we still had it; and in all the glorious and gaudy pageantry the proudest trophy, the foxtail, was ours."

Proud Ten kept the foxtail for many a day, by dint of many a famous run; but at last, in a cross-town fire, when several engines got bunched together, Seven Engine wrested it away.

Finally, the foxtail disappeared. Some say it was stolen by a hated rival; others, that it was ordered stealthily removed by Chief Scannell, who objected to it on the grounds of the fierce fighting it engendered.

It was never seen again; but Godfrey Fisher of Social Three, some years ago, noticed in a furrier's window a foxtail. He bought it, in memory of the old days, and had it mounted, flying upon a long stick on a base of mahogany. This he presented to the "Exempts" at the Admission Day celebration in Vallejo. And there it is today, the last feeble reminder of that once all-potent trophy.

# 15

# The Last Race

SENATOR HAWES, it so happened, was standing on the sidewalk that Sunday afternoon—December 17th, 1865—when the fight took place between Knickerbocker Five and the allied forces of Big Six and Social Three.

This fight did not, as is supposed by many, make directly for the bill creating the paid fire department. The bill had been pending for two years. At the time of the fight it was being fiercely debated in the Legislature, then in session at Sacramento. The fight merely served as a pretext for Senator Hawes to push the bill through the upper house.

Many of the Eastern cities had just recently installed paid fire departments. In fact, the volunteer fire department all over the country was fast dying a natural death. The telegraph alarm system was rapidly pushing the picturesque bell ringer out of his tower. Horses were supplanting running men, and steam engines were replacing the machines madly pumped by hand.

In San Francisco the citizenry, and especially the businessmen, who had been active in the department from the start, noting the signs of the times, began to withdraw in large numbers, and new men would not enlist. Many of the engines, thus left unmanned, were rendered useless, and the engine house, once a center of the social and political life of the city, became the rendezvous of the rowdy and the "runner," the man who paid no dues, did no work, assumed no duties, but just lounged about the engine house and ran with the machine for the mere excitement of it.

Notwithstanding all this, the passage of a bill killing the Volunteer Fire Department outright would, it was feared, produce a riot. The San Francisco Volunteer Fire Department was different from any like organization in the country. The reason was simple: San Francisco was a frontier town with a large mixed population, and it was separated from the rest of the world by a whole continent, by land, and two continents, by water. It was at the mercy of friend and foe. Its greatest foe was fire, its greatest friend the Volunteer Fire Department, which had given a service beyond price. In return, the people gave a love beyond measure.

Fast fading though its glory was, a few companies still remained active. Among these were Knickerbocker Five, Social Three, and Big Six, and between Knickerbocker Five and the other two there existed an old enmity. So it was that any and every action of Knickerbocker Five was sure to provoke vigorous opposition on the part of Big Six and Social Three. Scannell had been elected Chief by the New

York faction. This was legitimate cause for Big Six and Social Three straightway to agitate trouble for him on any provocation. For instance, one day at Washington and Dupont streets, for cause unknown, a member of Social Three pummeled Scannell to a finish.

Scannell had a habit of using strong language, especially under stress of great excitement. No offense was intended; it was merely his rough manner of expression, and was so understood by all the men. But Hossefross, foreman of Big Six, who had himself at one time held the position of Chief, made it on one occasion a pretext to stir up trouble for Scannell.

"Dutchy," said Hossefross to one of his green men, "did you hear what Scannell called you when he ordered you to go through that window? Well, if you don't make him apologize for those words or punch his nose, I'll punch your head." Trembling between fear of Hossefross and fear of Scannell, Dutchy timorously approached the mighty Chief. Hossefross, having scant confidence in Dutchy's prowess, came up from behind, seized his man by the nape of the neck, and shouted at Scannell: "You can't use any such language to one of my men without an apology. You apologize to him or I'll punch your head!"

The enmity between Knickerbocker Five and Big Six deepened when the Civil War broke out. Openly Southern in sentiment, Big Six now became silent. There were rumors that the Secession element had been secretly hatching a plot to carry California out of the Union. Knickerbocker

Five accused Big Six of being Secessionists and traitors. Every run to a fire was made an occasion for hurling abusive epithets back and forth.

On that Sunday afternoon of 1865 was fought the last fight of all. An alarm had been turned in from the box at Fourth and Mission streets. Engine Three came along down Sansome. As it turned into Market and Second, someone sang out, "Here comes Number Five!"

Engine Three had from thirty-five to forty men on the rope. Many were outsiders, for, as the custom was, the citizens ran with their favorite machine, as the spirit moved them. Fearful of a fight, these extra men dropped off, which gave a slack rope. Not wishing to be passed by Number Five, Three turned into Jessie, a narrow street, both its sides lined with wagons and carts. Knickerbocker Five followed close behind and, anxious to pass, endeavored to run Engine Three onto the sidewalk and capsize it. Two men of Engine Three, still on the run, jumped on top of their engine, and, armed with blunderbusses, fought off Knickerbocker Five.

Engine Three now turned into Third Street. The grade toward Mission was all downhill. Three made good time. Arrived at Third and Mission, it drew its rope across Third Street so as not to be passed by Knickerbocker Five. The street was black with men. Knickerbocker Five came along, a hundred and twenty strong, and attempted to pass. Three resisted. Five opened up an attack. Three, outnumbered, was knocked out; and Five dashed along Mission. One of the engineers ordered Three to go home, although, according to law, the men could not be ordered off the rope until after a formal roll call. Just as the men were about to comply, someone shouted, "Here comes Number Six."

Big Six, which had followed the route taken by the Knickerbockers, shouted jeeringly, "A nice lot of fellows you are!" Knickerbocker Five went out Fourth Street, with Big Six following on behind. Five continued on and made good time, but the fire was out. Returning homeward, it passed between the lines of Big Six and Social Three, still going in the direction of the alarm. Scannell appeared at this juncture and shouted, "Boys, go home; the fire's all out!"

Social Three, smarting under its defeat and itching for retaliation, lifted Scannell forthwith and deposited him upon the sidewalk. Deserting the ropes, the men of Six and Three jumped on top of the engines and, armed with blunderbusses, spanners, and crowbars, attacked Knickerbocker Five. Many of Five's men fled in terror, leaving the engine manned by few others than its officers. Presently all three engines were deserted, while the men fought in the middle of the street. Cobblestones were ripped up and used as missiles. Finally, in the midst of flying spanners, billets of wood, stones, crowbars, and blunderbusses descending on heads and shoulders, came a pistol shot—again—and yet again. Some say five shots were fired.

Ed Flaherty, assistant foreman of Knickerbocker Five, was shot, though not fatally, in the head and back. Another member was shot in the foot. George Stanton, of Big Six, was slightly wounded. All the men had black eyes and bloody noses and many bruises. Some had broken bones which laid them up for weeks in the hospital. Three of the twenty-five policemen who had been standing all the while on the sidewalk, powerless to interfere, now came up, and arrested George Stanton of the Monumentals, and Charles McMann, assistant foreman of the Knickerbockers, and two of his men.

Senator Hawes immediately sent word of the fight to Sacramento. On Monday morning, at the first session, the bill was passed.

Midnight of December 2d, 1866, was the hour set for the bell to toll the knell of the Volunteers. That afternoon, Broderick Engine Company, No. 1, marched to Lone Mountain Cemetery—once the *ultima thule* of the city, and now close to the heart of town—to unveil there a statue of its hero, Broderick. Lafayette Hose likewise marched to Lone Mountain to dedicate a full-length statue of its own hero. Big Six and Social Three planned to combine and for the last time to lay for Knickerbocker Five. A fire was staged to take place exactly as the bell should toll the hour of midnight. Relays were stationed at every block. Every man went armed.

At the stroke of midnight came the alarm of fire. Big Six sped away and out of its house in Brenham Place, passing the engine house of the paid Fire Department at Bush and Kearny before that company had its horses out. But a mistake had been made in the signal. The fire was staged for Fourth and Howard; the alarm struck Sixteenth and Howard, and Five Engine failed to turn out. This was lucky, for somebody would certainly have been killed.

Social Three, as befitted the founders of the first temperance organization,—the Dashaway Society,—went straight home, seeking consolation in sleep. Big Six lined up at the Snug, where Chris Buckley was tending bar that night, and wound up at Hess's place in Portsmouth Square, before turning into its engine house for the last time.

Three hours later a genuine alarm, for a fire in a fruit store at Second and Folsom streets, initiated the paid Fire Department into active service.

# 16

# Bella Cora

BELLA CORA was slight of build and a little above medium height. Her skin was as delicately tinted as the pink-white blossoms of the peach. Her eyes, changing with excitement from dark gray to hazel, were as lethal in their depths as the seed that comes from the poppy. Her form, in the perfection of its outline, was as beautifully seductive as the rose that unfolds to the full warmth of the summer sun.

She dwelt in the fashionable street of the half-world, Pike Street, which is Waverly Place today. Here, in the early 'fifties, could be found surprisingly beautiful women. They came upon the first announcement of the discovery of gold; tall, finely proportioned women, with brilliant, flashing eyes and dazzling white skins. Many of them were cultured; some were accomplished musicians, and some spoke several languages. Among them Bella Cora reigned as queen.

Among all the sumptuous houses in the street, hers was unequaled in luxury. The walls were lined with French satins and hung with mirrors and paintings that set off the wealth of velvets and laces in draperies, the heavy velvet of the carpets, the gilt of the chairs. The most noted men of the town, judges, lawyers, politicians, as well as the gay and gilded youths, attended in full force the great balls she gave twice yearly. The merchants bowed low when she drove up and stepped from her carriage into their shops. The people made obesiance, for her purse was ever open and generous to their charities. All homage was hers—so long as she observed the bounds fixed by polite society for women of the outer darkness.

But one day Bella Cora stepped boldly into the light where dwelt the women of the polite world. And by that single act she roused an angry sea that was to run red with the blood of men, and of the man she loved.

Bella Cora was the daughter of a clergyman of Baltimore. She was of part Irish extraction and went at times by the name of Arabella Ryan. She had not yet reached her eighteenth year when a young man, handsome and of engaging manners, captivated her eye, fired her imagination, and then betrayed her. When her secret became known to her father, he cast her out and closed his doors forever against her.

The girl went to New Orleans. There her baby was born; and there it died. She found herself one day alone, forsaken, the hand of the world against her, and down to her last dollar. Heavy at heart, knowing not which way to turn, she wandered to St. Mary's Market.

I have all this as Bob Hogan told it to me, a year or so before his death; just as he had it from Bella Cora herself, in those moments of deep confidence when the two sat together talking of the devotion each had for the man who had gone. Bella was Charles Cora's widow; and from the day that Charles Cora had rigged Bob up in a fireman's cap and cape so the boy might march as bravely as any man in the firemen's parade, Bob had been his devoted friend and admirer.

St. Mary's Market stood in Tchoupitoulas Street, by the Mississippi River. Its roof was of slates once carried as ballast in sailing ships, its flooring was of German flagstones. French Basques from the Pyrenees for years ran the meat and vegetable stalls. Italians had a section all their own. Indian women squatted on its flagstone floor, selling grass baskets and herbs, among them deerfoot, an herb for perfuming clothes. Negroes walked about selling pralines, a confection of New Orleans brown sugar and pecans from the trees grown in abundance in that region. Citizen and stranger alike came to St. Mary's Market, all day and all night long, to the marble-topped counters where drip coffee, famed the world over, was to be had—*café noir* and *café au lait,* with two large puff pastries, all for ten cents.

As the girl sat alone, forlornly sipping her coffee and taking a dreary inventory of her young life, she felt a pair of eyes upon her from a stall across the way, the eyes of a woman flashily dressed and bedecked with jewels. The woman came over to her.

"You seem lonely and sad," she said, smiling, as she seated herself beside the girl.

"Yes," replied the girl, "I am lonely, and I am sad."

"Perhaps you are in need of money," said the woman. "If so, I wish you would allow me to lend you some." At this kindness, the girl broke down and told her story.

"Perhaps," said the woman, when she had won the girl's confidence, "before you come to me I had better tell you who I am."

But the girl only laughed recklessly.

As the two went out together and across the narrow, cobbled street, two men were sauntering along the sidewalk opposite. One of them was a trifle above the medium height, slim and dark, with large dark eyes, dark olive skin, and a black mustache. He wore a white Panama hat, fashionable clothes, and fine patent leather boots. He was Charles Cora, the gambler. His companion was a dealer in a temple of chance.

"There go the two handsomest women in New Orleans," exclaimed Cora.

The dealer turned. Recognizing the older woman, he bowed to her, but did not lift his hat.

"You know her," said Cora, "yet you do not lift your hat?"

"Not to her kind; no."

"And who is the girl?" asked Cora.

"I don't know," said the dealer, "I never saw her before."

"Well, then," said Cora, taking a twenty-dollar gold piece from his pocket, "here's for the one to learn who the lady is."

He tossed up the coin. It fell to his lot. He crossed over. The woman's smile invited, but his large, dark eyes consumed the girl.

So it was that though she went with the woman to live in a fashionable street of the half-world of New Orleans, she knew no man but Cora.

In the gilded house of pleasure the merriment ran high. The wine sparkled. The shoulders of the young and beautiful women gleamed dazzlingly above their gorgeous gowns of laces and silks against the background of velvet hangings and mirrors. And when she saw the men who came and devoured these young and radiant creatures, her devotion to Cora for saving her from a like black destruction became a loyalty that was almost worship.

The announcement of the gold excitement in California startled New Orleans like the rest of the world. Friends of Cora told him of the wonderful opportunities in the gambling houses in San Francisco. When he finally decided to leave for the new field, nothing could persuade Bella Cora to remain behind; she sailed with him. Both of them were young and full of hope; he was thirty-three and she was twenty-two.

II

It was Thursday, November 15th, 1855. The Ravel family, with the Martinettis, were holding the boards of the American Theater in San Francisco.

From the oval dome of its interior, where a shining sun revolved inside a circular wreath of brilliant clouds, hung chandeliers scintillating with innumerable lamps of shimmering glass. The heavy velvet draperies of the proscenium boxes were supported from above by the beaks of gilded wooden eagles. The horseshoe tiers of boxes were like solid phalanxes of white pillars, outlined in gilt.

The cheapest-priced seats were in the pit; the choice seats were in the first balcony. At the back part of the pit, stalls fitted with velvet hangings were set apart for the demimondaines; they were never seated in any other part of the house.

The Ravels, who had come for a season's engagement, had been playing two weeks at the American. This Thursday the theater was crowded, for they were to put on for the first time a new play, "Nicodemus; or, The Unfortunate Fisherman."

The Ravels were masters of pantomime and had been creating a furor all over the world. They gave entire dramas without so much as uttering a single word, conveying by facial expression alone the most varied emotions. Charles Ravel was considered the handsomest harlequin on the stage. The Ravels had combined with the world-renowned Martinetti family of acrobats, who were to give, following the opening performance of "Nicodemus," the "Lutte de Pagela," and in conclusion the fairy extravaganza, "The Red Gnome."

All the brilliant, the noted, and the fashionable of the city were assembled. Seated in the first balcony was United States Marshal Richardson, with his wife and a lady of her acquaintance, who noticed a man in the pit gazing intently and persistently at them. So marked was his attention that the ladies became exceedingly annoyed, and General Richardson left his seat to go and learn the meaning of such conduct.

The glances, however, were not intended for General Richardson's wife nor for her friend, but for the woman behind them, Bella Cora, who was seated with Charles Cora, the gambler. An abandoned woman attending the theater, and seated in the audience! General Richardson, indignant, went to the foyer to demand that Bella Cora be summarily ejected. He was absent from his seat for some time, and greatly excited when he returned. He had to acknowledge a complete failure; and the defeat rankled. He, a Southerner and a Federal officer, publicly to have been triumphed over by a gambler, and that, too, when seeking to safeguard his own wife!

In an age of hard and fast social boundaries the line was much more sharply drawn, in all things, in the South than in the North. With negro slaves to do the useful work at his slightest bidding, the Southern white man had much more leisure to practice the arts of gallantry, and the Southern white woman the arts of helplessness—the "distinguishing marks" of the gentleman and the lady. To a Southern gentleman nothing lent quite so much distinction as an exhibition of prowess in defense of a lady; and nothing could be so humiliating as failure. Moreover, General Richardson's humiliating defeat would soon be the gossip of the town—among the theater parties, at the restaurants, in the groups at the saloons—for Richardson's voice had been none too gently modulated when he had made his demand.

Charles Cora was a gambler; but, as Bob Hogan says, "as straight as a string, and noted for his veracity and his courage"; and he held gambling to be a legitimate profession, since it was licensed by the State. He was amiable, peaceable, slow to anger, and slow to form friendships. Once he was aroused, he was an enemy at all hazards; once a friend, he was a friend at all hazards. He was more than a friend to Bella Cora.

Although she had come off victor in the encounter with Mrs. Richardson, Bella Cora smarted under the insult implicit in the demand for her removal; for she, too, was a Southerner, and the daughter of a clergyman. She felt herself to be, in family and breeding, the equal of Mrs. Richardson; she felt herself to be as true and faithful a wife to Charles Cora as Mrs. Richardson was to her husband; the single difference was that society had stamped its approval on the one union and not on the other.

The next afternon, as Richardson was going down the street, Charles Cora came by with some friends. Each was still smarting over the incident of the evening before. Cora, with a laugh, short and exultant, as Richardson passed him, flung upon the air a brief and stinging remark which on the instant leveled Richardson in his habits and profession little above the gambler himself, and held his wife up to the contemptuous pity of the community.

Later—a little past midnight—Cora was seated in the Cosmopolitan saloon, playing backgammon with an acquaintance, Dr. Mills, when Richardson entered with some friends. As yet the two men had never met by formal introduction. As Richardson stood now at the bar drinking a glass of champagne, Dr. Mills, hoping to repair the breach between them, brought Cora up and introduced him. Richardson invited them to join him in a drink, and the two, apparently on amicable terms, left the saloon together.

When they were outside, Richardson, by a simple, natural remark, gave Cora an opening which Cora could not resist, and again he flicked Richardson with the same stinging remark of the afternoon. The next instant, Cora rushed back excitedly into the saloon, Richardson following. Dr. Mills swore later, under oath, that "Cora asked, 'Have I any friends in this room? This man is going to slap my face.' General Richardson came in smiling and said, 'I promised to slap this man's face, and I had better do it now.' Some person then said, 'Oh, you mustn't do it.' And the thing was stopped. Some words afterwards occurred. Some persons proposed to introduce General Richardson to Cora again, but it was not done. I don't know why. I think the General was a little tight. Cora appeared to be sober."

Next day, as Richardson was about to leave his house, his wife, fearful that the matter might prove serious, exacted a promise from him that he would leave his pistols at home. By four that afternoon, Richardson was heavily under the influence of drink. While he was openly confiding to one and all his sense of humiliation, and vowing vengeance, he was met by his friend Dr. Poppy. Even more fearful than Mrs. Richardson of a possibly serious outcome to the affair, Dr. Poppy exacted a promise from him that he would return home immediately. This, with the easy promise of the man who is drinking, Richardson readily agreed to, only the next minute to turn down, instead, toward the Cosmopolitan saloon in search of Cora.

Failing to find him there, Richardson went down Clay Street, and encountered Cora walking with a man by the name of Ragsdale. Again there was a seeming reconciliation, the three settling the difficulty over a drink at Hayes' saloon, and again at the Cosmopolitan. But Cora did not share the optimism of Ragsdale; he had a vague sense that Richardson was not fully placated. Richardson was in a highly susceptible state, and likely to be swayed by any wild thought demanding action.

A brief hour or so later, between six and seven, Cora was in the Blue Wing saloon when a messenger brought him word that a friend was waiting outside who wished to speak to him. When Cora did not return, his friends went to inquire the cause. The street was seething with excited people. Richardson had been shot—dead. Cora was under arrest.

III

San Francisco in the early 'fifties was easily roused to mob action. The men were young and volatile, jostling each other daily in crowded streets, jammed together in lodgings at night, and living, day and night, in an atmosphere surcharged with the excitement of gambling in mines and at cards. Only a touch was needed to move them to violence. Richardson, prominent and popular, shot dead in a public street, supplied the touch. There was talk of lynching Cora.

Later that night the bell in the engine house of Big Six sounded a call to arms. Many who had belonged to the Vigilance Committee of '51, followed by an excited crowd, assembled at the Oriental Hotel, where Sam Brannan made a speech in which he called upon lynch law to make up for the inefficiency of the law of order. He was arrested, but immediately gave bail, returned, and again addressed the crowd.

Fifty armed men were placed on guard at the jail. The streets were alive with people, moving from the jail, where Cora was locked up, to the spot where Richardson was shot, and flocking in great numbers to view Richardson's body, which had been carried to the marshal's office in the Merchants' Exchange Building. By morning it was as much as a man's life was worth to espouse openly the cause of Cora. On all sides Cora was denounced in the most scathing terms. Some even said that Bella Cora had instigated the murder.

At ten o'clock on the Sunday morning a coroner's inquest was held. The room was thronged with spectators. The body was lying in an adjoining room, where people passed by it during the whole afternoon. Three derringers were exhibited upon the table; two of them had been taken from Cora, one discharged and the other loaded, and the third had been found, cocked but not discharged, near the body of General Richardson. The following verdict was returned:

"That the said William H. Richardson came to his death by a pistol shot fired from the hands of one Charles Cora on the night of Saturday, November 17th, between the hours of six and seven o'clock; that the said Richardson went, in company with the said Charles Cora, to a place near the corner of Clay and Leidesdorff streets, in the city of San Francisco, in front of a store occupied by Fox & O'Connor, and that the said Richardson was then deprived of his life, in the manner aforesaid, by the said Cora; and, from the facts produced, the jury believe that the said act was premeditated, and that there was nothing to mitigate the same."

The coroner's jury had not dared to render any other verdict. But I have it from Bob Hogan, as well as from the evidence showing the position in which the pistol was lying beside Richardson and the position in which the knife was found underneath the grating of the sidewalk where the struggle had taken place, that Richardson had not left his weapons at home as his wife had advised, and that Cora had knocked both weapons from Richardson as he drew his own pistol and fired in self-defense.

Bella Cora summoned the leading criminal lawyer in the city, Colonel E. D. Baker. Bob Hogan said that he named thirty thousand dollars as his fee and that Bella Cora counted out fifteen thousand in gold on the spot. When it became known that he had taken the case, a storm of protest descended upon Baker. Fearful of the consequences, he delegated his professional brother, Governor Foote, to return the fee to Bella Cora, and to announce his withdrawal.

As the newspapers tell the story:

"Governor Foote consented to undertake the disagreeable mission. The woman was immovable in her determination to keep Colonel Baker to his engagement. And she intimated, in terms not to be misunderstood, that she was determined that he should fulfill his obligation.

"When Governor Foote related to Colonel Baker the result of his mission, he advised the Colonel to see the woman himself. Colonel Baker went, Governor Foote accompanying him.

"The Governor later said he had never witnessed such a manifestation of a woman's power and irresistible influence. Bella Cora was inspired to the height of heroism in her devotion to Cora, her purpose to secure his acquittal and prevent his sacrifice.

"She first appealed, then implored, then begged Colonel Baker to stand by his engagement. He made no response. And then, he seeming not to yield, she commanded that he must! She would double his fee! She would have him appear as Cora's counsel if he did no more than sit in court with Cora near him and have it known that he was Cora's counsel. He must! He should! She was inflexible!"

On December 1st, "during the session of the Fourth District Court, Charles Cora was arraigned on the indictment for the murder of General Richardson. It had been kept profoundly secret that this judicial ceremony was about to take place, in order to avoid the collecting of a crowd and the excitement consequent thereupon.

"The prisoner was brought down by Sheriff Scannell and his deputy, Mr. Harrison. He was conveyed in a closed carriage, and the whole ceremony of arraignment in the courtroom was a matter of extreme privacy. Cora was self-possessed. He wore a richly figured velvet vest, and light sporting kids, and overcoat thrown lightly over his shoulder....

"Quite an array of counsel appeared in behalf of the prisoner—General McDougall, Colonel Baker, Judge Tilford and Colonel James."

On January 3d, 1856, the trial began.

"It was found necessary to station two officers, one at the door, and the other at the bar, to guard the entrance into the court and to keep back the crowd who were pressing forward in their anxiety to witness the proceedings.

"The prisoner, Charles Cora, was seated in a corner of the courtroom, attended closely by an officer. His appearance was very much changed since the first time he appeared at the bar of the court. He looked anxious and troubled, and seemed to take the deepest interest in the proceedings, so much so that he appeared to be scarcely sensible of the curiosity of which he was the object.... The expression of his face manifested anxiety, and, perhaps, a shade of terror, and his whole person betrayed nervous restlessness. Not the vestige of a smile passed across his face, although every person else was laughing and tittering at some ludicrous circumstance or witty saying. He sat alone in melancholy solitude, a deplorable reminder of the solemn and awful character of the occasion, which others, for a moment, seemed to have forgotten. Some say he wept while Baker was speaking of his protecting angel."

Daily he saw the wall which was to shut him off from all touch with his fellows mount higher and higher, built by the stones they threw at him—the mob, the daily papers, and, worst of all, the prosecuting attorneys. Richardson, a lovable man when sober, but dangerous when drunk, was depicted as a god, stainless of all sin; Cora, as the vilest of creatures, a man who lived off the earnings of a woman of shame.

This, I am told by Bob Hogan, was rank injustice; Cora never took a single cent from any woman, least of all from Bella Cora, until a fortune was necessary for the defense of his life. And what was life to her without him?

Inevitably Cora's friends fell from him. Every character witness, every intimate, no matter how near he might have been, was discredited on the ground merely that he was on Cora's side. His lawyers were defamed on the ground that their services were being paid for by an abandoned woman. And in truth she paid them well; she poured upon them money like water. That, again, was made a circumstance against him. When it was impossible to tear her from his side, they besmirched him with this loyalty as further indication of his own vileness.

The taking of testimony was concluded on Monday, January 14th. The next day Baker made his historic argument, with its passages of great sublimity, beauty, and pathos, which flowed without a break, like music from a tongue of silver.

The jury, after being out forty-one hours, sent two communications to the Court, asking to be relieved, upon the ground that after "deliberation upon the evidence of the case, without the possibility of agreeing, together with the fact that several of us are really suffering in health from privations unavoidedly incident to our situation, and that the business of others is suffering from their absence, warrants us in requesting and expecting our release."

The ballots stood thus. First ballot: six for murder; four, manslaughter; one, acquittal. Second ballot: murder, six; manslaughter, six. Third ballot: murder, seven; manslaughter, five. Fourth ballot: murder, eight; manslaughter, four.

Prolonged and angry came the murmur of the mob cheated of its prey. Cora was remanded to jail, to await his second trial.

IV

On May 14th, 1856, Charles Cora was in jail awaiting his second trial but confident of his ultimate release—as he had been ever since the disagreement of the jury. Toward sundown, suddenly he heard again the low, angry growl of a mob that is cheated of its prey. The next the now uneasy Cora knew, James P. Casey, under heavy guard, was brought to the jail and locked up for the murder of James King of

William, editor of the *Bulletin*. In tones from which all hope had fled, Cora said to Casey: "You have put the noose about the necks of both of us."

Casey was a young man of twenty-eight years, and a political power. He was known as an expert ballot-box stuffer and a desperate fighting man. In one memorable fight between Casey, Bob Cushing, foreman of Engine No. 11, and a man named Bagley, twenty shots were exchanged, and Cushing received eleven wounds—none of which, however, proved fatal.

It is said that Casey held office through his success at ballot-box stuffing. He had been inspector of elections in the Sixth Ward. This year he had been returned as county supervisor from the Presidio District, although he did not reside in the district nor was his name mentioned on the day of election as a candidate. Soon after his "election" as supervisor, he started a little weekly sheet called the *Sunday Times*. In the Volunteer Fire Department he was an active member of Engine No. 10.

Casey had been allied politically with the Broderick faction, but he had switched later to the Terry faction because of its Southern sentiment. The foreign element in San Francisco was for the most part in sympathy with the South. The Italian, Cora, who had lived much in the South, was therefore, with Casey, of the Southern political faction, which at that time was dominant in both city and State.

The dominance of the Southerners did not provoke any ill feeling beyond what might be laid to purely sectional prejudice. Hatred flared only after those concerted acts of the Northerners which history has commonly credited to the Vigilance Committee of '56.

It would have been impossible for three thousand men to form themselves within a few days into an efficient military and judicial machine. Some preparation must have been made. As a matter of fact, it had indeed been made; and, given an excuse, it would be manifested. The crimes of Casey and Cora supplied the pretext for which the power behind the Committee had long been looking.

The Vigilance Committee stopped neither murder, gambling, nor election frauds. What good it accomplished was in spite of its violence, not because of it. The good it accomplished was that the three thousand and more men who made up its membership, having previously shirked their civil responsibilities, now took an active part in the government for twenty years.

So long as the country was prosperous the respectable element concerned itself little with moral issues. The very men who formed themselves into the Vigilance Committee were, many of them, foremost in shirking their responsibilities as citizens. Many had joined military and fire companies solely to escape jury duty. The baser element held public office because most respectable men refused to go into politics.

The prosperity of the city began to ebb in 1854. The city began then to feel the cost of its many conflagrations, to which was added the heavy drain of municipal extravagance, the fleecing of the exchequer by local jobbery, and the robbing of the city by numerous schemes, notably that monstrous swindle, the Peter Smith water-lot sale.

The early spring rains had materially lessened the output of the gold diggings. Overbuilding had caused rents to drop. The merchandise which glutted the market was ruthlessly sacrificed. By the middle of the year, of a thousand business buildings three hundred were unoccupied. Then came the panic, in which many of the banks, representing the largest interests and the most numerous depositors, closed their doors. The first day of the crash, Friday, February 23d, 1855, was spoken of for years afterward as "Black Friday."

It was the Northern businessmen that were hardest hit; they had neither the wealth nor the political power of the Southerners. And looking toward possible recovery, they had less than nothing to expect from the slave power; their single hope lay with the government at Washington.

"At some points in the interior, especially Sonoma, San Joaquin and Visalia," to quote from a letter found among the belongings of the late Horace Davis, "the 'Secesh,' as we called them, were numerous and noisy, raising the Confederate flag, and even organizing military companies at one or two places. The country south of the Tehachapi, too, being largely Mexican, was willing to secede. But as long as the United States held San Francisco the malcontents could do little but bluster. San Francisco was the key to the situation on the Pacific Coast. Whoever held this city could control the Coast. Municipal government, as reorganized by the Vigilance Committee in 1856, was absolutely loyal to the Washington administration."

It was in the fall of the year of this great panic that James King of William published his initial number of *The Daily Evening Bulletin*. In two short months it had become a great power and had the largest circulation of any newspaper in the city. Its reputation was that of a heroic, idealistic, fighting journal. In the opening number King announced that, whatever his individual political bias, in his public capacity his aim was toward nonpartisanship—which implied, however, neither neutrality nor indifference—in matters of public concern; irrespective of party, he would advocate only such measures as might seem most conducive to the public good.

So true was the *Bulletin* to King's declaration that, as Hittell says, "those whom it attacked and those who knew that they were liable to be attacked, though they affected to despise it, were in constant dread and terror, and various plans were discussed as to how it might be muzzled or its influence destroyed. The only means was to get King out of the way."

Casey, according to Hittell, was urged by men higher up to make of a private grievance a pretext to kill King. A verbal battle had for some time persisted between the two men, Casey in his columns in the *Sunday Times* and King in the *Bulletin* each denouncing the other. Finally, in the afternoon issue of the *Bulletin* for Wednesday, May 14th, 1856, King wrote what proved to be his last editorial.

"It does not matter how bad a man Casey had been, nor how much benefit it might be to the public to have him out of the way, we cannot accord to any one citizen the right to kill him, or even beat him, without justifiable personal provocation. The fact that Casey has been an inmate of Sing-Sing prison in New York, is no offense against the laws of this State; nor is the fact of his having stuffed himself through the ballot-box, as elected to the Board of Supervisors from a district where it is said he was not even a candidate, any justification for Mr. Bagley to shoot Casey, however richly the latter may deserve to have his neck stretched for such fraud on the people."

Casey's prison record had long been an open book to San Francisco. His admission of the fact that he had served eighteen months in Sing-Sing had been published in all the San Francisco newspapers, and, at the time, he seemed to care little. But now he was up in arms.

About four o'clock that afternoon, almost immediately upon the appearance of the issue of the day, Casey, in search of King, appeared at the editorial rooms of the *Bulletin,* on Merchant Street, between Montgomery and Sansome. Casey's voice, in King's office, was heard above the editor's. He was apparently much excited, and he spoke as if short of breath. An hour later the whole town was seething with excitement. I give the statement as published in the *Bulletin* at the time, and as it was had from King himself.

"At a few minutes past five o'clock, Mr. King left his office, as usual, for dinner. He walked on the pavement in front of Montgomery Block, going northward. At the Bank Exchange, he crossed the street diagonally towards the Pacific Express office. Casey, who had been previously observed walking on the west side of Montgomery Street, opposite Montgomery Block, as if watching for King's appearance, was at this time on the pavement before the Express office. He was observed to step into the street as King crossed, and, suddenly throwing off a short cloak which he wore, presented a revolver at King's person, when he and King were only a few feet apart, and fired. The morning papers differ somewhat in their accounts of this attack—one asserting that Casey said, 'Draw and defend yourself'—another that Casey said, 'Are you armed? I am going to shoot you'—and at the same time firing. King did not hear any such words, nor had he the least notice to defend himself. He heard a noise like a person crying 'Come on!' or something like it, and at the very instant saw a pistol pointed at his breast, which was fired. The 'Come on' and firing were as closely simultaneous as could be. Mr. King, in the anticipation of death, has made this statement to the proprietors of this paper, and to the friends around his bed-side."

As another account takes up the story:

"Casey was instantly arrested, and locked up in the station house. The street by this time was filled with a wildly excited populace, running in every direction, cursing and crying, 'Where is he? Take him out! Hang him! Run him up the first lamp post!' It soon became known that Casey was at the station house. A rush was made by the crowd toward the City Hall. The officers, finding that greater safety might be obtained over the person of the prisoner, had him removed to the County Jail.

"At half-past six His Honor, Mayor Van Ness, appeared at the jail and tried to counsel the crowd to wisdom. But his voice was drowned in cries of 'Where is Cora now? Hang him! Down with justice! Hang him!'

"From seven to eight o'clock Montgomery Street from California to Washington was the most crowded public thoroughfare ever witnessed. It was estimated that no less than ten thousand persons were present. Several speakers appeared on a balcony and encouraged the people by flaming appeals to avenge the blood of their fellow citizens who had fallen. One speaker then proposed that all should go home and arm themselves and meet at the plaza at nine o'clock.

" 'Go into the Pacific Express office,' he said, 'and see upon the floor the life blood that has flowed from your fellow citizen and swear upon that blood that it shall be avenged.'

"At the appointed hour the plaza and avenues about it presented a thrilling scene. The excitement was intensified when it became known that the Vigilance Committee was assembled in the Pioneer clubrooms.

"During the whole of the evening one living mass of humanity was moving from the jail to the place of shooting.

"That night, the entire population seemed to have gone to bed whispering King's name, blended with Casey's, upon their lips."

Nor did the Committee allow the excitement to die down. It was to their interest to keep it fanned.

At 11:30 o'clock, a mounted battalion prepared to stand guard throughout the night over the city.

V

Early Thursday morning, thousands filled the street in front of the City Hall, where the Vigilance Committee was recruiting its forces, but no one was allowed to enter the Council Chamber unless vouched for by some member of the Vigilance Committee of 1851.

Merchants who refused to enroll were whipped into line by threats of withdrawal of credit and supplies, or even of attachment. In a single day the *Herald,* which in the morning had come out with a denunciatory editorial, was reduced from forty columns to twenty-four. The *Herald* was the favorite organ of the Democracy, of the anti-Broderick and Southern wings particularly.

By Friday, Sheriff Scannell—the military having declined to respond to the call of the authorities to protect the jail—was forced to lay in an extra large number of guns and to call upon volunteers for assistance. How desperate was his need is evidenced by the tender age limit in his call for recruits.

STATE OF CALIFORNIA,<br>County of San Francisco.

To ——, a male inhabitant of said County, and above fifteen years of age:

Whereas, I have good reason to believe that a serious Breach of the Peace and Riot are to be apprehended, and that an organized attempt will be made violently to wrest from my custody a prisoner committed to my charge for safe keeping:

Now, therefore, by virtue of the authority in me vested, and in the discharge of my duty as Sheriff of the County of San Francisco, you are hereby commanded to be and appear at half past three o'clock, P.M., this sixteenth day of May, A. D. one thousand eight hundred and fifty-six, at the Fourth District Court room, in the City Hall, in the City of San Francisco, to aid me in the execution of my official duties in the premises.

DAVID SCANNELL
Sheriff of the County of San Francisco.

At the appointed hour the courtroom was well filled. Attorneys especially were represented. Many, however, had not, upon roll call, the courage to respond openly to the sheriff's call for assistance.

By Saturday the Vigilantes numbered twenty-six hundred men, organized into companies of one hundred each and equipped with shotguns, knives, and revolvers, two thousand muskets, and a fieldpiece.

On Saturday, Governor J. Neely Johnson came down from Sacramento and gave the Committee the entering wedge for which it had been waiting. The Committee had kept a deputation on constant watch outside the jail. Now, by order of the Governor, who, after much counsel with its executive body, had finally given way, the Committee was allowed to place fifteen of its armed men within the jail. And all day long every boat brought reinforcements from Sacramento, Redwood City, Folsom, Nevada City, Marysville, and other towns of the interior.

By Sunday the 18th the excitement had given way to a "solemn stillness." The people had begun to realize the nature of this thing they had evoked in their too eager thirst for vengeance. For the first time, on this Sunday, the physicians held out hope for King's recovery. But to the Vigilance Committee a delay in order to await the outcome might mean failure for its already determined purpose. So, at an early hour Sunday morning, orders were given to the commanders of the different companies to appear with their forces at the general headquarters of the Committee, No. 41 Sacramento Street, and to be ready for duty at nine o'clock.

At ten o'clock a hundred men, armed with pistols and knives and dispatched in small squads as scouts, advanced stealthily upon the jail from different directions.

At eleven o'clock a brass six-pounder, guarded by a great company of men in military array, moved along Sansome Street and was planted in front of the jail.

And now began the steady tramp of feet, the glint of many muskets moving from Kearny, Stockton, and Dupont streets toward the jail. They marched silently—not a word, not a sound save the reverberation of their rhythmic tread. As the account continues:

"By one o'clock the troops were all in position and prepared for action. On the south side of Broadway, facing the jail, they stood in triple line, supporting the brass fieldpiece in their center, which was loaded, with linstock alight. To the west of this a solid column was formed on the center of Broadway; upon the east were long lines extending to

Kearny Street; the same were carried through Hinckley Place, and surrounding the jail on all sides. Small detachments were stationed on the adjacent housetops overlooking the jail, and on the rear every approach was strongly guarded. The men were planted with military precision and the effect was that of an actual siege.

"The Vigilance Committee, having withdrawn from the interior of the jail, as agreed, the executive committee demanded entrance. They were met within by Sheriff Scannell, who was supported by deputies, a small posse, and police.

"Previous to this demand the knife and fork were removed from Casey's cell. The president of the Committee made a formal demand for the possession of Casey. The sheriff promptly acceded, stating that he was in his cell.

"The president entered. In the presence of those around him, Coleman informed Casey of the purpose of his visit.

"Casey expressed his willingness to go, and requested that he might have a fair trial and not be dragged through the streets. This was assured him.

"He was then handcuffed by Marshal North, and, in company with two of the Committee and the marshal, the latter at Casey's request, he was conveyed to a carriage placed in front of the jail door.

"Before leaving the jail a letter was handed to Sheriff Scannell informing him that the Committee would return in an hour for Cora. The carriage was then surrounded by a heavy detachment of troops and proceeded to and through

Kearny Street to Pacific, and through to Montgomery, up to Sacramento, to the Committee rooms."

At three o'clock a demand was made for Cora; Scannell flatly refused. A parley ensued; Scannell held firm. Orders flew without. The six-pounder was primed for action. The linstock was fanned into flame. A line was opened between the gun and the door. Would the streets run with blood? And now Governor J. Neely Johnson stepped forward. He counseled with Scannell, urged him not to resist. At this advice from the man to whom he had every right to look for support, Scannell, the fearless one, burst into tears.

Cora was allowed time to make his will, and to write a few letters of farewell.

At a quarter past four a carriage was drawn up in front of the prison and surrounded by a guard similar to the one which had conducted Casey. The subcommittee of the executive committee brought Cora forth handcuffed. He was dressed with extreme neatness and appeared composed. He was placed in the carriage, which, surrounded by the main body of the troops and with the fieldpiece in front, moved slowly down Dupont Street to the Committee rooms. As the carriage started off, there came the loud, despairing cry of Bella Cora: "Good-bye, Charlie. I have done all I could to clear you."

## VI

On Tuesday, May 20th, James King of William died, at 1:30 P.M. "The stores were immediately draped in mourning. Saloons and all public resorts were closed. Flags were placed at half-mast. Men placed bands of mourning on their left arms. All throughout the afternoon the deep tones of the bells tolled the death knell. Men stood in single file, the length of Montgomery Street, waiting their turn to ascend to the room in the Montgomery Block to view the remains. As the long line entered by one street, a long line left by the exit on Merchant. The talk was of nothing but the probable acts of the Committee."

Wednesday, May 21st. "A gloomy day, with sky overcast. The rain poured down. Business was almost entirely suspended, and the dreary aspect of the city was heightened by the symbols of woe which everywhere met the eye. As usual, armed bodies of citizens paraded the streets, horsemen galloped about in every direction. Everybody gave utterance to his sentiments in subdued tones, and everybody felt that a reign of terror had commenced. A revolution had taken place."

No man dared raise his voice in criticism of any act of the Committee, without danger of arrest. The arrests were made without warrant, oath, or responsibility. James Herbert, foreman of Ten Engine, of which Casey was a member, was arrested and locked in a cell at Fort Gunnybags for making the remark that "the Vigilantes were about hanging Casey for what they were doing themselves—taking the law in their own hands." A party of gentlemen who met quite by accident at dinner in a restaurant expressed freely their opinion of the illegality of the Vigilance Committee; the restaurateur was notified that if those gentlemen were allowed to assemble again the place would be closed. Judge Daniel J. Murphy, for nine years the district attorney, lived long to tell of his immediate arrest for merely calling out, at a mass meeting held on the pavement in front of the Montgomery Block, to an inflammatory remark made by one of the Committee's members, "That is not true."

On this same day, it is chronicled: "The woman, Bella Cora, was down on Commercial Street yesterday, manifesting considerable excitement as to what was to be done with the prisoners. She did not apply for admittance to the Committee rooms." Thursday, May 22d, the day of King's funeral, dawned clear and bright. By noon the sun beat down with all the intensity of summer. Over the city there hung, like a pall, the black of mourning. Every business house, every private dwelling, especially along the streets through which the funeral procession must pass, and even the ships on the Bay, were draped in black. Flagstaffs were draped with crape, and every flag was at half-mast—except one, the flag of Ten Engine, the fire company to which Casey had belonged.

Business was entirely suspended. The solemn stillness was broken only by the sound of the hammer at Fort Vigilance. Two rows of cells were being built for the ever-increasing number of prisoners who had incurred the displeasure of the executive committee. Two platforms were being constructed for the doomed.

Bella Cora only that morning had got wind of the secret—that Cora and Casey were to hang as the hearse bearing

King's body should round the corner where, on Tuesday, King had breathed his last.

The previous Sunday, when the two men had been removed from the jail by the armed forces of the Vigilantes and transported to the upper rooms of the Committee's headquarters at Sacramento and Front streets, they had at once been arraigned before their self-appointed judges. The mode of trial was of necessity primitive. Casey was merely taken before a subcommittee, by whom his testimony was put in writing. He was then turned over to the executive committee, to see whether his oral statement agreed with his affidavit. With Cora the procedure was equally simple. It consisted in reading to him the evidence of his trial in the Fourth District Court.

Judge Daniel C. Murphy, who sat through every day of that trial, has told me that the evidence was preponderantly in favor of Cora's having shot in self-defense. Many men of high character, on that evidence, had deemed Cora not guilty, and so, too, had part of the jury. Free law acquits whenever it doubts. By the constitution of the Vigilantes, a two-thirds majority could inflict the death penalty.

Rumor had it that the execution would be stayed at least till Friday, the day after the funeral. Even the newspapers—by this time all, except the *Herald,* under the control of the Vigilantes—seem to have had no other information than current talk. Only the members of the executive committee and the officers in charge of the funeral cortege, who had equipped themselves with field glasses, were in the secret that the execution was to be made a part of the funeral ceremonies.

The mass of the people, thinking the funeral was to be the main event of the day, had flocked early that morning to get places of vantage. Long before the services began, the Unitarian Church was crowded to suffocation, and every available spot on the pavements, in the windows, on the balconies, and on the hilltops along Stockton, Washington, Montgomery, and Bush streets, the route the procession must take to Lone Mountain Cemetery, far out among the sand dunes, was jammed. With so much secrecy had the executive committee surrounded its actual intentions that, except for those of their own organization who were needed to guard their fortifications, the water front, where Fort Vigilance was situated, was almost deserted.

VII

Fort Vigilance, or Fort Gunnybags, as it was sometimes called, occupied the block bounded by California, Sacramento, Front, and Davis streets, at that time within a few blocks of the Bay. On the ground floor, it embraced half a dozen stores of the Truett Building. The second floor extended nearly halfway of the block, as connections had been made by cutting doorways into several of the adjoining buildings.

On the ground floor were the fieldpieces and heavy ammunition, and the small arms arranged in racks. On the second floor were the rooms for the heads of the departments, the executives, and the several inferior officers, and the cells for the prisoners. The executives' room was profusely decorated with flags.

At the front of the block, all along the main entrance, which was on Sacramento Street, about ten feet from the buildings and extending nearly to the middle of the street, gunnybags filled with sand had been piled five feeet high. At either end of this fortification were two pieces of artillery. The rear entrance to the second-story rooms, which was approached by a small street cut into the center of the block from Davis Street, was likewise fortified with gunnybags filled with sand.

A narrow passageway through this fortification admitted the members to the enclosure and thence to the building. Guards with muskets and fixed bayonets stood on duty day and night in the two narrow passageways to the doors on the lower floor and all along the stairway leading to the rooms above. They were stationed at the foot of the stairs, midway of the stairs, and at the top of the flight, before every door and every room, and in the passageways leading to the different rooms.

A large triangle hung from the roof of the block to sound the call to duty of every member at any time, day or night; also, a seven-hundred-pound alarm bell belonging to Big Six; and several cannon were placed conspicuously upon the roof.

The usual guard around the rooms of the Committee had been secretly augmented at an early hour that Thursday morning. Cavalry paraded the four streets enclosing the building, and several companies of infantry guarded the entrance to the Committee rooms, from Front to Davis and on Davis Street from Commercial to Sacramento streets. The roofs of the entire block bristled with bayonets. The fieldpiece which the Committee had used in its attack on the jail was planted in front of the room, ready for action. Above all came the sound of the carpenters' hammers.

It was 12:30 o'clock, just about the time when King's funeral procession was being marshaled in front of the Unitarian Church on Stockton Street. Suddenly, from the direction of Sacramento Street, a hack came at breakneck speed. It halted in front of Fort Vigilance. A woman, heavily veiled, alighted. With head erect and all defiance in her manner, the woman brushed past the guards in front as if they did not exist. With winged feet she sped along the enclosure to the door leading to the stairway. On, up, she flew, past bristling bayonets and muskets, to the very door of the star chamber, with so brave an air that the guards in wonderment fell back.

She entered the executive room. She threw back her veil. It was Bella Cora. Her face, her whole being, breathed defiance. Her eyes glowed dark in her anger and her scorn of the men, seated, secure in their virtue, at a long table, above which, from the wall, hung two large American flags.

At her entrance a hush fell upon the room. Hushed was the little crowd without, waiting expectant in the broiling sun. Not a sound, not a breeze to disturb the stillness—only the ring of the carpenters' hammers, building two scaffold platforms for the two men.

Throughout the past days—in fact, ever since that fatal day in November when Cora had killed General Richardson—Bella Cora, in fear of jeopardizing his welfare by her presence, had held herself in the background. All through the trial, when it would have been her joy to be seated daily in the courtroom, to encourage the man she loved, never once did she put in an appearance. Instead, she curbed her eagerness for knowledge of the day's doings until court adjourned.

All through those long days when he languished in the county jail, awaiting his second trial, she had been happy. Was he not alive? Could she not look into those eyes, troubled and anxious, but to her always tender and kind? She could care for him—bring him food prepared by her skilled colored cook. She could look to his cravats and his frilled shirts and his fancy waistcoats—that they should all be of the richness and exquisite neatness his fastidious taste demanded. Over all was the happy hope that he would soon be free! Then came this dreadful thing—an armed force to wrest him from his security in the jail, and to bring him to an unjust, unlawful, unrighteous, cruel end.

All these thoughts welled up within her and added to her anger. What availed pleadings from such as she to them! Not a ray of sympathy could pass from their hearts to her.

Pale, but angry and defiant, she stood now. Her eyes blazed black in their scorn.

They would hang him like a dog, the man she held dearer than life. They would make his loved name a by-word. Well, she would defy them. Henceforth she would wear that name as her crown of glory.

The Church requires for marriage but the assent of both parties, a written contract or merely a letter. But she commanded them to fetch a priest and to lead her straight to Charles Cora, in the presence of witnesses and in the sight of God to be united to him, that she might legally bear till her last breath the name of wife.

Father Accolti was already with Cora in his cell. That much mercy had been shown him—as also to Casey. A hurried summons, a half-hour before, had been made for the spiritual advisers of each of the doomed men.

Cora was, as always, carefully and neatly dressed. Outwardly he was calm and composed. His only sign of emotion was the frequency with which, in his last moments, he pressed to his lips the crucifix he held in his hands.

And so they were married at 12:30 by the clock. She remained there in his cell to the last, clinging to him, with eyes haunted with tears. It was light and darkness about her at the same time.

It was 12:45 by the clock. From the committee room two small platforms were passed through the windows, to extend about three feet in front of the building. Two beams were shoved from the roof, from which dangled two ropes, each with a noose at the end. Other ropes were attached to the platforms and fixed with springs. The men braced themselves as they tautened the ropes to make the platforms swing level with the iron doors.

One o'clock! Suddenly the stillness was broken by the solemn toll of the church bells. The services for James King of William were over. They were carrying his body to the hearse. The heart of Bella Cora went cold within her. Frantically she clung to her husband. She kissed his eyes, his lips, his face, his hands.... Men came to take him away.

Ten minutes past one! A white paper fluttered from the committee room to the guards below. It was an order to present arms. The next instant Charles Cora, a white handkerchief bound about his face and tied around his neck, his arms pinioned to his sides, his feet bound with cords, was shoved out on the east platform. The noose was adjusted. Like a living statue he stood there.

Casey walked out of the window on the west platform. His head was bare. He held a white cambric handkerchief in his hand. He looked pale and his eyes were bloodshot, but the mask of determination was on his face. The noose was slipped about his neck. He whispered a few words to Father Accolti, who stood by him. The priest requested that the noose be removed to allow Casey to say a few words.

"Gentlemen," Casey began, "I have been persecuted most relentlessly by the *Alta,* the *Chronicle* and the *Globe.* I hope these editors will desist and allow my name to pass into oblivion and not publish it as a murderer. I have an aged mother in the Atlantic states and I hope the steamer papers will not send my name to her as a murderer. Gentlemen, I am not a murderer. I did not intend to commit murder. I do not feel afraid to meet my God on a charge of murder...."

Casey's speech lasted seven minutes. All the while Cora stood silent and still.

Casey retired now a few paces inside the building. The rope was adjusted around his neck. A white cap was placed over his head. His arms were pinioned at his elbows. His feet were bound together with cords. He shuffled himself forward on the platform like a blind man groping in the dark. He still held his white cambric handkerchief in his pinioned hand.

It was 1:21 o'clock, precisely. Suddenly, to the tolling of the church bells, came two loud, sharp taps of the bell on the roof of Fort Vigilance. The men below uncovered their heads.

At the second tap, the platforms were pulled suddenly away. The two figures swung round two or three times in mid-air. The handkerchief that Casey had been holding fluttered to the ground.

## VIII

The coroner, fearful of what the mob might yet do, removed the bodies of Cora and Casey from Fort Vigilance by strategem: he had two empty coffins taken out by the front door and placed in his wagon; two others, containing the bodies, he caused to be carried out by the back entrance almost unobserved.

After the inquest, Bella Cora demanded as a widow's right the body of Charles Cora. She summoned the most skilled embalmers. She bought a coffin of heavy mahogany, trimmed in silver. She sought the padre of the Mission Dolores for a burial plot. Friday the body lay in a small house occupied by her colored servants, on Broadway, between Stockton and Powell streets, and Bella Cora watched it there through the night.

That same day, the following paragraph appeared in the *Daily Alta California:* "It is rumored that Belle Cora, the widow of Charles Cora, has received a communication signed by the Committee of Citizens, in which she is charged to make preparations to vacate the house she now occupies, by the first of June, as the Vigilance Committee are making preparation to compel her to leave town." The newspaper attempted further to discredit her by stating that she had been forced to marry Cora, the priest refusing otherwise to grant final absolution to the doomed man, and that she had complied angrily and defiantly with the executive committee's command for her presence. The *Bulletin,* however, expressed the deepest sympathy, and spoke of how "the unfortunate woman clung to her husband to the last moments of his life," and how she "now clings to his remains with all the devotion of her sex."

On Saturday, only a small crowd watched the little cortege that moved from the house in Broadway to the Mission Dolores. The hearse was drawn by four black horses, and was followed by a train of seven carriages. In the first rode

Bella Cora with her women friends; the next carriage contained her colored servants, and the other five were filled with the men friends of Charles Cora. The last rites were said in the church. The coffin was lowered into the earth in the churchyard adjoining, and flowers were strewn upon the grave.

Two days later, Monday, May 26th, this letter appeared in the daily papers:

To the Vigilance Committee:

Allow me to express to your respected body our high appreciation of your valuable services so wisely and judiciously executed. You have exhibited a spirit of forbearance and kindness that even the accused and condemned cannot but approve. May Heaven continue to guide you.

But, gentlemen, one thing more must be done: Belle Cora must be requested to leave this city. The women of San Francisco have no bitterness toward her, nor do they ask it on her account, but for the good of those who remain, and as an example to others. Every virtuous woman asks that her influence and example be removed from us.

The truly virtuous of our sex will not feel that the Vigilance Committee have done their *whole* duty till they comply with the request of

Many Women of San Francisco.

But the Vigilance Committee seems to have paid no heed. Bella Cora remained, till her death, in her house in Waverly Place. She lived alone, but for her servants. She dressed in the deepest mourning. She spoke of herself never otherwise than as the widow of Charles Cora. She attended faithfully the services at St. Francis' Church. Always noted for her generosity, she now became doubly generous with her charities. An admiration for her replaced the earlier scorn.

On Wednesday, February 17th, 1862, she died. A few years before, finding that the Mission cemetery had become crowded, and would not permit of her lying beside the man she loved, she had had the body of Cora removed to Calvary Cemetery. The stone which marks her as his wife she had engraved before she died.

Bob Hogan once took me on a pilgrimage to the graves. He had taken a day off from the District Attorney's office. He was soberly arrayed in his best suit of broadcloth, and had gathered a branch from his drooping pepper tree to lay in tribute on the stone. Beneath two eucalyptus trees, we came to the burial plot, its coping sunken and covered with stray leaves and ivy. The headstone, which stretched the width of both graves, was engraved with two figures—a young man and a young woman—standing with heads bowed, under a weeping willow tree.

# 17

# The First Entertainer

SAN FRANCISCO'S first entertainer, Stephen C. Massett, was the true Bohemian type. He was an artist, with an equal capacity for work and diversion, whose ruling principle was, "If your pocket is light make your heart light to match it; if your coat is torn, laugh while you patch it."

Massett was "a red-faced little Englishman" with a wealth of copper-colored curls, a heavy mustache and goatee, a face full and mobile, with the nose of the philosopher and the eyes of the dreamer. He was poet-actor, song and dance artist, composer, essayist, lawyer, auctioneer, notary public, and "wandering minstrel in many lands." He was best known to San Francisco as "Jeems Pipes of Pipesville," his *nom de plume* as a writer of humorous prose. It pleased Mr. Massett, after his characteristic vein of humor, to call Pipesville a "ranch," but in reality it was "a little house not much larger than a full-sized Saratoga trunk" in a bog near the "bridge" on Mission Street.

Massett came to this country by sailing vessel from England in 1837. He articled himself in Buffalo, as a law student, where to "an occasional line of Blackstone, a half-page of Kent, or a speech of Charles Phillips," he devoured Shakespeare, "learning 'Richard III' by heart, a portion of 'Othello,' and a scene from 'Macbeth.'" Finally, concluding that his chances of becoming distinguished at the bar were slim, and not being able to penetrate at all into the mysteries of Coke, Kent, or Blackstone, he drifted. He eked out an existence in countinghouse and theater, as clerk, bookkeeper, salesman, wandering minstrel, from New York to Boston, to Charleston, back again to New York, to the Mediterranean, to Malta, Constantinople, and returned once more to New York, there to remain four years as clerk in the law firm of Brady & Maurice.

It was while he was living in Charleston, Massett confesses, that "happening to fall in love with a large pair of dark eyes, I gave vent to my feelings in the words and music of a song—my maiden effort—'When the Moon on the Lake is Beaming.'"

A victim of the gold fever, Massett set sail by schooner for San Francisco in January, 1849. He was eight days crossing the Isthmus by muleback, jolt, bump, jolt, across streams and hills, into bogs and holes and out again. Then, for thirty days he was becalmed on the Pacific, in dreadful heat, and with malignant fever among the passengers. The horror seemed never-ending. The ship was ninety-eight days making its way from Panama to the Golden Gate.

This awful journey, this need for some less perilous mode of travel, later inspired Massett to compose the stirring music of "Clear the Way." More than any other one thing, it is said, "Clear the Way" helped to create public sentiment in favor of a transcontinental railroad.

CLEAR THE WAY; OR, SONG OF THE WAGON ROAD

*Words by Charles Mackay* *Music by Stephen C. Massett*

(Composed for and dedicated to the Pioneers of the Great Pacific Railroad)

[The first stanza only is given here]

Men of thought, be up and stirring, night and day;
Sow the seed, withdraw the curtain,
Clear the way!
Men of action, aid and cheer, as ye may;
There's a fount about to stream,
There's a light about to beam,
There's a warmth about to glow,
There's a flower about to blow,
There's a midnight blackness changing into gray,
Men of thought, and men of action,
Clear the way!

On the morning of the ninety-ninth day after his departure from Panama, Massett set foot on the shore of San Francisco, then a city of tents and wooden shanties. The first man he met was Colonel J. D. Stevenson, whom he had known slightly in New York. Stevenson, who had been in command of the California regiment of volunteers which left New York for the Mexican war in 1846, had on several occasions visited the law offices of Brady & Maurice, where Massett was employed.

The Colonel was now a "land commissioner," though he could never quite live down his military past; he still habitually wore a closely buttoned frock coat and military fatigue cap. According to Massett, the Colonel was pretty smart when it came to disposing of his real estate, which was somewhere in the mosquito-infested, malarial marshes not many miles out from Sacramento. The dodge was "forfeiture of the lot" if a house were not erected in thirty days. Lumber was difficult to get, and the houses that were said to be coming by way of the Horn never arrived.

The Colonel, learning that Massett had no definite object in coming to California, but was just drifting about, suggested that he come the next day to his office. "You are just the young man for me," he said. "You of course understand drawing deeds, mortgages, *et cetera;* in fact, the general routine of a lawyer's office. I have just purchased a tract of land—am going to build a new city—a second New York, sir! I call it, sir, 'New York of the Pacific,' sir! I'll make you Alcalde, sir! Notary Public, sir! Mayor of the city, sir! Come and breakfast with me, sir, tomorrow."

"At what time, Colonel?" asked Massett.

"At six o'clock, sir—always rise with the lark," replied the Colonel. "There is nothing like getting up early, sir—businessman, sir. Go to bed early—keep steady—don't drink, and your fortune's made in no time!"

The next day, Massett, after breakfast with the Colonel, went to his office, a wooden shanty, with a door that opened with a rusty old latch, and just behind the door a wooden bunk. Here, at high tide, the water came up to the doorsill, so that, as Massett later used to say, "I had to wade up to my middle to get into my crib."

The office, we are informed in Massett's *Drifting About,* was on Montgomery, between Washington and Jackson streets.

"The walls were adorned with large maps, most gorgeously got up," by one who was to be Massett's fellow clerk, a brother Englishman named Row. "The desk was a long deal board, relieved at intervals by two old tea cups, both full of ink, and paper and pens; by its side, a cupboard, with two or three nameless utensils filled with gold dust; three wooden stools, very shaky and rickety—and the fixtures and furniture are complete.

"On the outside the people were informed that that was J. D. Stevenson's Land Office and Agency of Lots in New York of the Pacific. Immediately under this they were now to be informed that Stephen C. Massett was a Notary and Commissioner of Deeds."

Massett, however, was not long to be left undisturbed over any "arduous task" in the real estate office on Montgomery Street. It soon became noised about that the red-faced little Englishman with the shock of copper-colored curly hair was a whole company in himself. A show in San Francisco! The intelligence rivaled a gold discovery. Straightway a clamor for a show arose that nearly swept Massett off his feet, and soon the announcement of the opening show, on June 22d, set the town agog with excitement.

ON MONDAY, A CONCERT WILL BE GIVEN
AT THE
COURT HOUSE, PORTSMOUTH SQUARE
BY MR. STEPHEN C. MASSETT
Composer of "When the Moon on the Lake is Beaming" and other Popular Ballads

PROGRAM

| | |
|---|---|
| 1. Song | "When the Moon on the Lake is Beaming" (Words and Music by S. C. Massett) |
| 2. Recitation | Mr. Massett. The Frenchman, the Exquisite and the Yankee in *Richard III* |
| 3. Song | Mr. Massett. "My Boyhood's Home," from the Opera of *Amilie* |
| 4. An Imitation | of Madame Anna Bishop in her song of "The Banks of Guadalquiver" |
| 5. Song | "When a Child I Roamed" (Words and Music by S. C. Massett) |
| 6. An Imitation | of an elderly lady and a German girl who applied for the situation of soprano and alto singers in one of the churches in Massachusetts. S. C. Massett |

PART TWO

| | |
|---|---|
| 1. Song | Mr. Massett. "When Time Hath Bereft Thee," from *Gustavus III* |
| 2. Mr. Massett | "Loss of the Steamship President," by Epes Sargent |
| 3. Mr. Massett | "I'm Sitting on the Stile, Mary," by W. T. Dempster |
| 4. An Imitation | of the N. Y. Razor Strop Man—John Smith |
| 5. Ballad | "She Wore a Wreath of Roses" (Mr. Massett) —J. P. Knight |
| 6. Ballad | "List While I Sing," composed by Stephen C. Massett |

7. YANKEE IMITATIONS "Deacon Jones and Seth Slope," S. C. Massett

8. TO CONCLUDE with the Celebrated

"YANKEES' TOWN MEETING

in which Mr. Massett will give imitations of seven different persons, who had assembled for the purpose of "SUPPRESSING THE PRESS"

Tickets $3 each, to be had at Dr. Robinson's, Chemist and Druggist, on the Plaza; at the Parker House, of Mr. Bassett; at the office of Col. J. D. Stevenson, and at the door on the night of the performance.

N.B.—FRONT SEATS RESERVED FOR LADIES!

Neither money nor pains were spared to make the evening a success. A piano—the only one in the State—was lent for the occasion by Mr. E. Harrison, Collector of the Port; it was moved from his office to the courthouse across Portsmouth Square, at a cost of sixteen dollars. This act was typical of the generosity of spirit that was to mark all the activities of San Francisco in the years to come. Massett fared not nearly so well in other sections of the country.

"I had a melodeon in those days," relates Massett, "as pianos were difficult to obtain, upon which I accompanied myself in my songs. Now this has not a very lively effect upon the performance, or the audience—the music emitted therefrom being a sort of cross between the accordion and a barrel organ. At the same time I have to keep the wind up by a perpetual movement of the right foot on the pedal. If for a second I miss, the bellows indignantly resigns its office. The machine gives a feeble and dying squeak, and I am left to the tender mercy of my audience.

"It was during a very pathetic rendering of the opening song, 'When the Moon on the Lake Is Beaming,' that this fatal casualty happened, and to add to the miserable state of my feelings—which I trust will be fully appreciated by the reader—I was requested to 'dry up' by some one in the pit.

"Now, whether this suggestion had anything to do with the hydraulic nature of the ballad in question, I know not, but considering it was only the commencement of a two hours' performance, I think my situation deserved some sympathy."

Massett modestly called his performance a "concert," and conducted the entire evening's entertainment single-handed with such marked success that the more skeptical among the audience disputed earnestly whether he was in reality, as purported, one man, or a whole troupe.

Varying fortunes and his habit of drifting about found Massett acting as auctioneer at Sacramento, and again as a "wandering minstrel," touring the mining and agricultural towns of northern California and Oregon. Of that tour, he recounts a pleasant evening spent at Grass Valley with Lola Montez in her "picturesque little villa guarded by a large-sized bear, sundry dogs, parrots, cats, etc."

His permanent abiding place, however, for many years was his beloved so-called ranch of Pipesville. It became famed the country over as the "poet's corner," the rendezvous of Bohemians like himself, whose art was greater than their recompense, yet who never failed to match their light pockets with still lighter hearts.

# 18

# The First Playhouses

WHEN Monterey and Sacramento had already seen the light of Melpomene's torch, San Francisco was still in darkness. In fact, the first dramatic performance in San Francisco was owing to a visit by the company from the Eagle Theater at Sacramento. And Downieville, though the *ultima thule* of California, was yet, to the actor, second in profitable importance after Sacramento.

Monterey, as was to be expected of the first capital of the State, had the first theater. The building, erected in 1848, may be seen today, half adobe, half frame, with a pit, a room to the side with a fireplace, and a stage shut off from the main part of the house by a wooden partition hung on hinges, which evidently served as a sort of drop curtain.

By the fall of 1849 Sacramento had celebrated the opening of the Eagle Theater, its first building to be dedicated exclusively to the drama, with a performance of "The Bandit Chief; or, The Forest Spectre."

On January 16th, 1850, the Sacramento company gave San Francisco its first evening of the legitimate drama, with the presentation in Washington Hall of "The Wife" and "Charles II." Before this there had been only the ballad concert of Steve Massett and the circus performances of Joseph Rowe, whose big tent was pitched on Kearny Street near Clay.

Immediately after this successful opening performance in Washington Hall, Rowe hastened to build a stage in his amphitheater and to begin a dramatic season that included a change of bill almost nightly. Matinees were unknown, but the evening performances lasted until midnight, the program often including both play and afterpiece. Here is an illuminating list, gleaned from the diary of J. M. McCabe, who was an actor in the pioneer company of both the Eagle Theater and Washington Hall, of the performances given at Rowe's Amphitheater in 1850, in the month of February alone:

February 2. "Intrigue; or, The Bath Road."
February 4. "Bachelor Buttons" and "Othello."
February 7. "Dead Shot" and "Love in Humble Life."
February 8. "Tinker, Tailor, Soldier, Sailor."
February 13. "Idiot Witness."
February 15. "Race for a Wife" and "Seven Clerks."
February 16. "Irish Tutor."
February 19. "Golden Farmer."
February 20. "Happy Man."
February 21. "Lady of Lyons."
February 23. "William Tell."
February 27. "Rent Day."

The March bill opened with "Richard III," with Mr. Nesbit McCron as Richard.

By November, Tom Maguire had opened, over his Parker House saloon and gambling place, his first Jenny Lind Theater, where James Stark, the tragedian, played the leading roles in such plays as "Damon and Pythias," "The Merchant of Venice," "Macbeth," and "Virginius." The Jenny Lind Theater was not, as so many have supposed, the outcome of an appearance here of the great singer. Jenny Lind never came to the West. But at the height of her career there was a rage for naming everything after her.

This first Jenny Lind Theater, opened in October, 1850, was destroyed by the fire of May 4th, 1851. On June 13th, Maguire reopened in a new building, only to lose it in nine days by the fire of June 22d. With money from the sale of the ground where it had stood, with unlimited credit, and with a confident anticipation of immense rentals, he then put up a handsome brick building—which, on August 15th, 1853, he sold to the City of San Francisco for two hundred thousand dollars for use as a city hall.

Innumerable minor theaters—the Phoenix, the Athenaeum, the Italian, and the like—sprang up overnight, to live for a brief season, a performance or two, and then to be heard of no more. All these so-called theaters were merely rooms or halls, or rude temporary structures with the crudest of accommodations. Often, like even the Jenny Lind, a "theater" was incidental to a gambling house or saloon. They were dreary places in fine weather and almost uninhabitable in wet. Twenty-five to thirty of them were destroyed by fire, some before the opening night.

What the legitimate theater did not have to contend with from without, it suffered from within. A chronicler of the 'fifties writes: "The pioneer company that gave the initial performance in Washington Hall was under the direction of Messrs. Atwater and Madison and consisted of Mr. Atwater, Mr. Daly, Mr. Wright, Mr. McCabe, Mr. and Mrs. Rowe, and others whose names are not remembered. The performances were not of a very high order, but drew houses for several nights, when the establishment burst up in a professional row....

"In the month of March of the same year [1850], Mr. Rowe, who had a circus in Kearny Street, fitted up his establishment for stage performances and engaged a company which had shortly before arrived from Australia and consisted of Mr. and Mrs. Hambleton, Mr. and Mrs. McCron, Mr. and Mrs. Batturs and others.

"Heavy business, a very heavy business, was done here for a while to good houses, when Mrs. Kirby, now Mrs. James Stark, arrived and commenced a star engagement. She at once became exceedingly popular and attracted crowded houses for some time, when a professional row occurred, commencing with Mrs. Kirby and Mrs. McCron, and the company was broken up."

The theater had also to struggle against the competition of the gambling houses, where entertainments were given which in seductiveness left little to be desired.

The best houses and the best business locations in the city were reserved for temples of chance, some of which paid a daily rent of more than five hundred dollars. Dazzling lights from glittering chandeliers shone upon walls handsomely frescoed and hung with mirrors and choice paintings, and on rich appointments of mahogany and velvet. Bands of music played; Ferrer, the renowned guitar player, could be heard; Strauss waltzes enchanted the ear; there were singers, or, as in the El Dorado, minstrel shows and vaudeville, and Mexican señoritas who nightly danced the fandango. Masked balls and parties were of frequent occurrence. And all this was free—whereas at Rowe's Amphitheater you shivered in the cold at five dollars for a box seat, three dollars for one in the pit, and fifty-five dollars for a private stall. And, too, the god of chance beckoned on all sides to faro, roulette, and monte. At one table, in 1850, two millions in gold dust and coin is said to have changed hands every month. How baleful the spell, the following excerpt from McCabe's diary will show.

"1850, January 16.—Opening night of company from Eagle Theater, Sacramento.

"January 23.—Closing performance; the treasurer, Mr. Mattinson reporting 'No salary,' he having lost the entire week's receipts at monte."

The city called loudly for some place of amusement to keep the young men from spending their evenings at the gambling houses. Fifty thousand dollars was subscribed, and a delegation of citizens, headed by Sam Brannan, called upon Dr. Robinson to see if he would build and take charge of a theater. The outcome of the negotiations was the "original" Adelphi Theater, on the west side of Dupont Street between Clay and Washington, a frame structure erected by members of the theatrical profession and opened in August, 1851, by Robinson & Weisenthal.

The first American Theater, built under the direction of Dr. Robinson, was opened at Sansome and Halleck streets in the fall of 1851. There were two American, two Metropolitan, and three Jenny Lind theaters; for what the fire did not destroy, the "made" ground did. The first American Theater was built on the insecure foundation of newly filled-in ground. At high tide the water rose several inches along the entire length of the passage, and entrance had to be effected by a footpath of planks, raised on stools or "horses." The second American Theater was built on the site of the first, which had been pulled down to give place to a handsome new structure.

Torrence, Dr. Robinson, Orrin Dorman, Weisenthal, John Fairchild, the scenic artist, and Jerry Bryant formed themselves into a stock company for the building of a theater exclusively for minstrel performances. Torrence owned the lot; he was also the stage carpenter. They built a one-story structure large enough to have a dress circle, and opened with the Bryant Minstrels. Their fortunes fluctuated, and finally, when the panic of 1855, with its bank failures, overtook them, Dorman and Bryant sold out to Tom Maguire. He enclosed the one-story structure in a three-story building, and changed the name of "Bryant Minstrels" to "San Francisco Hall." Later, he purchased the whole building outright, enlarged it, and named it "Maguire's Opera House."

Torrence, besides his numerous other interests, became proprietor of the Metropolitan Theater, which opened in December, 1853, with J. B. Booth, Jr., as stage manager, and Catherine Sinclair, wife of Edwin Forrest, as lessee. In respect to acoustics and view of the stage, the Metropolitan Theater far surpassed the American.

These two theaters, the American and the Metropolitan, together with San Francisco Hall and Maguire's Opera House, exerted a strong influence on pioneer theatricals. Indeed, to them is owing much of the golden era that was to come.

# 19

# The First Singer

THE PIONEER of musical art in San Francisco was Elisa Biscaccianti, the American Thrush. She was the first singer of any magnitude who dared come to this distant musical field, where Catherine Hayes, the Swan of Erin, feared to venture, and P. T. Barnum would not risk his Jenny Lind, the Swedish Nightingale.

In order to understand fully the great social service that Biscaccianti rendered to San Francisco when she undertook to bring her art to the Pacific Coast, one must have some real appreciation of the problems which confronted the pioneers in their attempt to reduce the chaotic condition of the times to some semblance of social order. They had solved the problem of the saloon by an appeal to standards. Likewise for this problem of entertainment they sought a solution, not by laws, but in some counter-attraction which should offer all the seduction of the gambling den without its destructiveness—without the quarrels, the shooting scrapes, the all-too-frequent suicides when high hopes were dashed to blank despair by a turn of the wheel.

They decided on the drama. But the path in this direction was strewn with difficulties, what with mud and fire, bleak theaters and cheap actors, and the general contrariness of the female sex. The theaters were swept away by fire almost as soon as they were built. The actors were second rate, for no artist of note would make the long journey by way of the Isthmus when the financial outcome was so uncertain. As for the ladies—what few the city boasted—they refused to sally forth unless arrayed in all the trappings of civilization. The mud, which seemed in those days to be independent of wet weather, all too often reduced attendance to a minimum. There was mud everywhere.

"From the Point to the sandy eastern suburbs of the city there is one vast fathomless sea of mud," an editorialist complained, "and from the water's edge to Portsmouth Square men and animals struggle and flounder and splash and spatter. . . . Its composition is heterogeneous, its character anti-pellucid, its adhesive qualities immense and antagonistic to a composed state of the nerves. Its ingredients are dust and water, egg shells, cabbage leaves, potato parings, onion tops, fish bones, and other articles too numerous to mention. Mud is the element in which we are now compelled to exist. It is utterly impossible to do anything without thinking of mud, to go anywhere without stirring in the subject, for, sober or muddled, a man is sure to put his foot in it. It is in every street, and a man is crossed by it at every crossing."

If mud made faring forth by day an undertaking, it made going abroad at night, especially to theater or party, a rough adventure. Gas was fitful, uncertain, and expensive. The few lamps along the Ambrosial Path were mainly in front of saloons and gambling dens, put up by their proprietors.

In the early 'fifties men stumbled to theaters at night by the glimmer of lanterns, proceeding cautiously along the unpaved streets, treacherous with holes and excavations, and along the plank walks, dangerous with loose nails and ill-fitting boards. In the rainy season, they sat wet and shivering in a cold theater. Naturally, the men chose the warmth of the saloon and gambling den, and the women refused to turn out at all. Carriage hire cost two dollars and a half, and was to be thought of only for great events.

The St. Francis, the first fashionable hotel of the 'fifties, attempted to solve the problem of evening amusement with the introduction of a series of soirees, of which it hoped to make a permanent social institution. There had been various earlier attempts at balls and parties—fancy-dress balls at the Bella Union, balls given by the California Guards, and the like. The Oriental Hotel, frequented by the army and navy set, had given a series of subscription dances. But the largest number of ladies at any of these affairs was twenty-five!

Previous to this, the St. Francis had but one social event of any importance, the banquet on its opening night, December 15th, 1849. (Parenthetically, this hotel was the first to put sheets on the beds. The city, theretofore, had been accustomed to sleep between blankets.)

The first soiree, which was given in June, 1851, showed an increased number of ladies, and at the July soiree all dreams were transcended when no less than sixty attended. This was epoch-making, and became the talk of the town! The press complimented the St. Francis on its great social service. At the September soiree, however, there were only forty couples, and, what was worse, a larger attendance of gentlemen than could be accommodated either with partners or seats at the banquet.

"Never did the St. Francis present such a brilliant scene as on the night set apart by our gentlemen to respond to the happy compliment paid them by the ladies of that elegant and fashionable hotel, a month since, in the entertainment given in the true spirit of a terpsichorean fete. The party of Thursday was creditable alike to the managing committee and the proprietor of the St. Francis, while it paid a merited honor to the fair under whose auspices the previous soiree was arranged.... The ladies of San Francisco never appeared to more charming advantage ... our gallants have been richly paid for all the care exercised in getting up the St. Francis soiree."

The Monumental Engine Company, Big Six, not to be outdone (they had a passion for being the biggest, the best, the first in all things), gave a grand ball, exquisite beyond compare in the decorations, the music, the ices and pastry. As for ladies, the St. Francis with its record of sixty was thrown utterly into the shade by the record of the Monumental, of FIVE HUNDRED ladies! Just where the five hundred came from is, even to this day, shrouded in mystery. A stringent rule, it seems, had been made that no gentleman could enter the ballroom without a lady. All California was ransacked. Some maintain that the ladies were brought, by pony express, from as far east as St. Joseph, Missouri.

Next day, the Monumentals were acclaimed the saviors of San Francisco's social progress, and the press declared happily that at last "the elements were resolving themselves into social order." But, alas, the event proved merely a flare. After this, social events, as well as the theaters, languished. The press inveighed to no avail against the lack of interest in the drama, which, "properly guarded and nourished," was "the helpmate of morality and virtue." Men refused to guard and nourish it in wet, cold, bleak weather. The press sighed in vain, also, over "the monotonous scene of breeches . . . but NOT A SKIRT!"

Social intercourse settled down chiefly to morning visits and an occasional luncheon with a few friends, women among themselves. Dressmaking was too expensive, dressmakers were too scarce, and material too costly to warrant the enthusiasm and expense incidental to the making of party dresses, except for the most momentous events. What could be done to bring back The Drama and Society? Men were disposed to patronize the theaters. That had been demonstrated—in dry weather! There were women in San Francisco to make up social parties. That, too, had been demonstrated—by the ball of the Monumentals. How to convert an event into an institution?

In the midst of their perplexity, and at the height of the season for mud, rain, and colds, the month of February, 1852, Elisa Biscaccianti stepped from the steamer, petite, lustrous-eyed, in the prime of her beauty and her voice, fresh from her recent triumphs in the States and in Europe. And what the St. Francis Hotel had tried and failed to do, in its series of soirees, toward the refinement of a frontier community; what the Monumentals had essayed in their own slashing ball; what the exhortations of the press in daily editorial had not effected, the wondrous voice of Elisa accomplished in a single night.

No longer did the press bemoan the "monotonous scene of breeches." No more did the women care about the high cost of dressmaking or the scarcity of dressmakers. Each one strove, at any cost, to outshine the others in sartorial splendor as they crushed into Sansome and Leidesdorff streets for the Biscaccianti concerts at the American Theater. No more talk was there of mud, no more complaints of excessive carriage tariff. The demand for vehicles far exceeded the supply. Those who were compelled to walk did so blithely, in fair weather or foul. And this, though everybody seemed to be suffering from colds that season, even the noted singer herself.

In a single night a frontier town had accepted the refinements of an Old World civilization. Alike to the miner in his rough flannel shirt and the dandy in his finery Biscaccianti seemed, in the words of the men of the times, a "singing dream that witched their homesick hearts back into a life of domestic joys and affections and social refinements long ago sacrificed and abolished."

Elisa Biscaccianti was born in Boston of an American mother and an Italian father. Her mother was the sister of the poetess, Miss Hewitt; her father was distinguished for his high musical attainments. Her education was the best that Boston could give, supplemented by tuition in the great musical centers of the Old World. She was a coloratura soprano, with a voice of surpassing delicacy. Her success, both in the States and in Europe, had been instantaneous. In Paris, Milan, Florence, London, and St. Petersburg she had created a furor in "La Sonnambula," "Norma," and "Lucia di Lammermoor." She was likewise famed as a singer of English, Scottish, and Irish ballads. Many discerning critics deemed her superior to Jenny Lind, while others declared her "not equal in fullness, sublimity, and inspiration to Jenny Lind, but surpassing her in pathos, truth, storms, melody, artistic finish, and high culture."

Her first concert was given on March 22d, 1852.

"At last she came forth and the moment the ardent multitude perceived her coming down the stage the greatest excitement was manifest. As she came forward to the footlights and bowed, round after round of applause greeted her. She smiled her thanks and bowed again. More applause. Another smile and an imploring look from her fascinating and speaking black eyes—thunders of applause—and so it continued for some minutes until the more sedate began to fear that the interchange of civilities would never end.

"She had selected the recitative and aria from Donizetti's 'Linda di Chamouni.' As her first notes rang out clear and distinct as a bell, the enthusiastic house was hushed into profound silence. Thunders of applause, showers of bravas and bouquets greeted the conclusion. Again she bowed her thanks, and again the audience was electrified by her sweet and expressive smile.

"For encore she seated herself at the piano and sang 'Home, Sweet Home' with embellishments, beneath a garniture of brilliant and varied ornament of rich brocades covered with point lace."

Her singing of the celebrated finale from "La Sonnambula" created as great a furor as she had ever excited in Europe.

"She seemed to have brought all her energies of mind and body to the task, and when at last she uttered, with a gush of melody, 'Ah, non giunge!' the house was electrified into breathless silence, following with strained sense through the wonderful and gorgeous reflections of the song as she revelled amid the tremulous and ecstatic tones of the cadenza. Twice was she encored and twice did she repeat the favorite melody."

The next day the people went about in a daze, and even the most sober-minded and judicial subscribed to the decision of the press that "the evening marked an era in the musical, social, and fashionable progress of the city."

After her fourth concert, the critics exhausted their superlatives, asserting that her voice could satisfy "the finest perceptions of the most musical soul with tones of as perfect sweetness and delicacy as it will ever hear this side of Gabriel's trump."

In none of her concerts did Biscaccianti "sing down" to her audience. She gave them the full complement with which she had gratified the most discriminating musical gatherings of the Old World. And they rewarded her, night after night, by an attendance which abated nothing in "the very élite and fashion of the city" that had greeted her at the *première*. If anything, their ardor increased with each concert. They "showered her with flowers as if to make her queen of the flowers." They besieged her carriage after the concert, escorting her back to the Oriental Hotel. This caravansary, because she stayed there, was to be the rendezvous for the great artists that followed in her wake. At the hotel they showered her anew with flowers. The fire companies came out in full uniform to honor her. On behalf of the Sansome Hook and Ladder Company, Captain Green's little three-year-old son, dressed in full fireman's regalia, placed a bouquet of moss roses in her hands. They proclaimed her the "Columbus of the Musical Pacific," lauding her as the first "to brave opinion and try her fortunes on the far shores of California."

With the exception of brief concert tours, Biscaccianti remained in San Francisco the better part of a year. She sailed for Lima in February, 1853. The fashionable of San Francisco flocked to bid her good-bye. The people would never forget her!

She returned to San Francisco in 1859. She had "placed a girdle of melody around the globe." In Lima she had "cast in the shade all the triumphs of Jenny Lind and Fanny Elssler."

The city of tents and shacks to which she had said farewell had become within six short years a cosmopolitan city, second in theatrical importance to New York alone. And for this remarkable transformation Biscaccianti, more than any other one person, deserved the credit. So, naturally, her heart overflowed with unwonted joy at this surprise. San Francisco had vowed never to forget the debt of gratitude it owed her. With the glorious fruits of her daring manifest on all sides, how much more glorious than on her first visit must now be its welcome to her. But her return made hardly a ripple on the smooth current of events.

Scarcely had she departed in 1853 when she was supplanted by Kate Hayes, the Swan of Erin, who was rushed in by a press agent who shrewdly exploited to the full the profitable field that the daring Biscaccianti had opened to the musical world. A few held out for a while in gratitude and loyalty to the American Thrush; but, though Kate Hayes was a ballad singer with neither the voice, the style, nor the culture of Biscaccianti, even these few went down before the conjury of the press agent. P. T. Barnum was said to be behind the Kate Hayes management. How could a simple-hearted and open-pocketed public help itself?

All this, Biscaccianti was to learn before she was many hours in the city. And more; where once her concerts commanded five dollars, three dollars, and two dollars, and crowded houses, she now aroused little enthusiasm at one dollar. San Francisco was satiated, gorged, with amusements of all sorts.

It so happened that George Evans, a pianist and conductor of note, was Biscaccianti's accompanist that season. He was said to be the actual author of "Dublin Bay," although another was given the credit. He was a young man, and fascinating; her husband was a man much older than herself. She left her husband and went to live with Evans. She also took to drink. From the concert stage she descended to the cheap variety house, the Bella Union, where she sang for nearly three years before she left San Francisco forever. By many she is remembered not as the first great singer the city ever knew, but as "Biscaccianti of the Bella Union"!

# 20

# The First Press Agent

NO SOONER had La Biscaccianti demonstrated that money was to be made in this frontier town, and by the best of art, than San Francisco sprang into world fame as the actor's El Dorado. The city was now overwhelmed with attractions of all sorts—ballets, operas, opera-ballets, symphonies, tragedies, comedies, farces, oratorios, pantomimes, panoramas. Junius Brutus Booth came, with his son, and James Murdoch, Matilda Heron, Catherine Sinclair, the Bateman children (infant prodigies), and the dancing Guggenheim sisters. Concert-givers came: Bishop, the singer, with Bochsa, the harpist; Madame Thillon, singer; Miska Hauser, violinist; Maurice Strakosch, pianist. Kate Hayes came, and carried away with her, it was estimated, close to a quarter of a million dollars. Lola Montez cleared sixteen thousand a week. Ole Bull expected to fiddle himself a million to recoup his losses in a recent speculation; he had been fleeced out of much of his savings by a company of real estate sharks, through a scheme to set up a Scandinavian colony in Pennsylvania. But with Strakosch and Stark, he came too late for the big money. The people were already satiated. Moreover, Ole Bull failed to maintain his reputation. He was criticized as playing skillfully but mechanically, and as "playing down" to his audiences. Accustomed by now to artists at their best, the people resented the fact that Ole Bull so frequently played, as part of his repertory, "Yankee Doodle" and the "Carnival of Venice."

Catherine Hayes was the first to introduce operatic scenes in costume, and firemen's benefits, to the theaters of San Francisco. She arrived virtually unknown. She departed an honorary member of the Fire Department, and took with her a small fortune in money, innumerable valuable presents of jewelry and gold slugs, a free steamer passage outward bound, a massive gold cardcase from the Irish, and the hearts of the entire population. But then, she had a press agent. His name Bushnell—W. A. Bushnell.

Catherine Hayes had a high soprano voice and a birdlike trill; some called her the "Irish Linnet." She was tall and blonde, with radiant, fair skin, and sparkling blue eyes. She was modest withal, yet with archness to render her seductive.

On November 20th, 1850, she arrived in San Francisco in a wild downpour of rain; and, worse luck, on the steamer "Oregon," which brought the first intelligence of the death of Daniel Webster. It would take the newspapers several days to recount Webster's life and deeds and give all the minute details of the obsequies, in columns lined in deep mourning the full depth of the page. What chance of public notice, then, had a songstress, however beautiful?

It was midnight when she set foot on the dock, and there was no one there to meet her, not even a carriage to convey her to her hotel. She made her way in the rain and mud to the Oriental, with only her faithful agent, Bushnell, as her escort.

Across from the Oriental Hotel was the engine house of California Four. Its lights gleamed in the darkness and the wet. The voices of the young men who crowded about the glowing fire rang upon the night air. Bushnell had some knowledge of the ways and doings of volunteer firemen. In the darkness he smiled.

Early next morning he paid his respects to the assistant foreman of Empire Engine Company, No. 1. Now it was the custom in San Francisco, on the day preceding a theatrical performance of any importance, to auction off the seats, in public, to the highest bidder. Miss Hayes' third concert was to be the great event, but Mr. Bushnell did not propose to trouble himself with anything so insignificant as a single seat. Nothing short of a box was to be auctioned off as the first choice. Furthermore, it was agreed between the assistant foreman of California Engine Company and the enterprising press agent that this first choice box was to be kept in the Department.

On the day of the auction the greatest excitement prevailed. The bidding rose rapidly from $50 to $500, and then, amid the cheers of an audience almost as large and enthusiastic as that present later at the concert itself, Captain George W. Green, in the name of the Empire Company, bought the best box seat for $1125, and paid $300 additional for choice parquet seats. Captain Green had been prepared to bid as high as $3000 if necessary. With the exception of $1300 paid by the Sutter Rifles for the first ticket at a subsequent concert in Sacramento, this is said to be the highest price paid for a single box in the history of concerts.

"The concert," writes the chronicler of the period, "was the engrossing topic of the day. At half-past seven o'clock Empire Engine Company, in full uniform, filed into the theatre, marching to the music of a fine band, and escorting the ladies, for whose occupancy the stage box on the left had been bid in by the Company, at the sale on Friday. This box was tastefully decorated with banners and insignia of the fireman, as was the parquette, where the members assembled in large numbers." In the box, as guests, were the governor of California and Mr. George Hossefross, of Monumental Six, then Chief of the Volunteer Fire Department.

Such enthusiasm! Each number was "vociferously applauded." At the close of the "Irish Emigrant's Lament" the house rocked with the thunders of applause. Miss Hayes was brought back again and again, to be showered with huge bouquets of flowers. Then, at a signal from the foreman, every member of Empire Company rose to his feet, and from a hundred throats, as one, came three ear-splitting cheers. After the concert, the members of Empire One, marching at the front and the rear of the carriage with torches flaming, banners flying, and the brass throats of their instruments blaring triumphant music, escorted Miss Hayes to her hotel, and bade her good night again in three tremendous cheers.

The town was hers! A few days later, a benefit for the firemen's charity fund was announced. The choice of seats for this benefit was bid in by Sam Brannan for $500, with other premiums as high as $700. This was the beginning of a charity fund for the volunteer firemen and their families, which, when the Department was mustered out, amounted to $105,000.

Never had the women turned out for the theater in such numbers as now. The daily papers recounted the unusual fact with surprise and pleasure. The merchants beamed. The shops were crowded with women buying satins, laces, gloves, and slippers. The men, not to be outdone, made equally lavish purchases of frilled shirts, scarfs, and fancy waistcoats.

Daily the critics reiterated their praises of the singer. They wrote of her "grace and becoming dignity." They raved over the "tender woe" of her "Irish Emigrant's Lament," the "exquisite pathos" of her "Savoureen Deelish," the "most captivating *espièglerie* and archness" of her "Comin' Through the Rye"—this song was her favorite encore—and "Kathleen Mavourneen," a new song just out. Nightly the applause increased. Fifty-dollar gold slugs rained down upon her, together with bouquets of flowers. On one occasion a gold slug hit her conductor in the heel as he was leading her, amid tremendous enthusiasm, off the stage. Another night a loud cry went up in the parquet, "From Calaveras County," and a huge bouquet sped through the air to drop at her feet. Attached to it was a jewel of great value.

The Irish, "anxious to testify appreciation," gave her a gold cardcase as "emblematic of our own green isle and the land of your sojourn." The contemporary description of the cardcase reads: "of pure California gold, massive and highly ornamented with designs emblematic of Ireland and California. It is in the form of an oblong square, its sides and edges flat and beveled to admit of engraving. On one side is engraved the Irish harp, surrounded with a wreath of shamrocks, tied with a scroll bearing the motto, 'Cead Mille Failthe, Kathleen Mavourneen' (a hundred thousand welcomes, Kathleen, my darling). Under the harp is an Irish wolf dog in a crouching attitude. Over the harp, on a scroll bedecked with flowers, is one of Miss Hayes' favorite ballads, set to music with words, 'Savoureen Deelish.' On the reverse side are depicted scenes illustrative of California from its primitive days to the present—a camping scene showing miners at work, excavating, pumping, fluming, and the like, and a view of Nevada. On a shield in the center is engraven, 'Miss Catherine Hayes, from a few of her countrymen, residents of San Francisco, February 5, 1853.' Around the edges are chased in relief sixteen designs of Indians, native Californians, miners, grizzly bears, wild cattle, etc."

When Bushnell announced that Miss Hayes was to appear in a season of opera scenes in costume, the critics broke all bounds. Her pathos now had become "sublime." She "charmed and electrified" her audiences by "the ringing melody of her notes." But a public letter, signed "Many," rebuked the noisy applause of the audience and the "indiscriminate and vulgar laudation" of the critics, and "called attention to the example of the most enlightened audiences of Europe, remarkable for the dignified and subdued manner in which pleasure is evinced." However, the applause abated not one whit, and even on nights of driving rain standing room was taxed to the utmost and disappointed throngs were turned away.

Then Bushnell announced a series of "final farewells." Those were happy days of many postscripts. The steamship company had already tendered her a free passage to South America, and the vessel was to sail on the Wednesday. On the Monday, the firemen turned out to give her a grand complimentary benefit concert.

"The theater was splendidly decorated with the insignia of the engine companies, the whole Department being present with their families, and from pit to dome the house presented a brilliant array, . . . noble-looking men in the uniform of their companies. . . .

"Besides these, there was a dense crowd outside the theatre, holders of 'pavement tickets,' who satisfied their desire to hear what they could of the great artist through the open windows of the building. . . . She was cheered repeatedly with 'three times three,' the whole Department arising to do honor in appropriate style and vehemence.

"After the concert her carriage was besieged with crowds of friends, which finally gave way to the ranks of the firemen, who, in full uniform, with torches and military music, escorted her to her hotel, where, from the balcony, she saluted them with an agreeable and appropriate speech."

In the unpublished diary of J. H. McCabe, there is the following entry concerning Miss Hayes' career: "1857—September—Sometime, during this month, married her agent, Mr. W. A. Bushnell, East."

# 21

# The Musical Idealist

WITHOUT symphonic music no city can boast a high musical culture. The pioneers aspired to the best, but artists of eminence lingered too short a time for the development of the highest public taste. However much gold might be showered upon them, artists could not be induced to remain for long so remote from the centers of world culture. But the gods lent a hand.

Traveling with Kate Hayes, under contract to Barnum to serve throughout the tour as accompanist and pianist, was a young man, twenty-five years of age, with coal-black hair and piercing, magnetic eyes—one Rudolph Herold. Herold had sat at the feet of the immortal Mendelssohn. He was imbued with a passion for the highest and noblest expression of his art. Gold, that spoke not the language of his art first, spoke not at all to him. At best he understood little of its language. Armored in his lofty idealism, he was safe from the prickings of avarice—but not from

Cupid's darts. He fell desperately in love. He broke his contract with Barnum, tarried to marry, and, tarrying, became the founder of symphonic music in San Francisco.

Of all the artists who visited this Coast in the pioneer period, none was more fit to become the father of musical culture and education in San Francisco, none more versatile or more profound in his art. Moreover, to his musical accomplishments he added a genius for organization. He was not only the founder of the symphony concerts, but also founder, leader, and teacher of all the early singing societies.

With Henry Meiggs, Herold founded, in 1854, the Philharmonic Society, the first vocal and orchestral organization. At its opening performance, on January 10th, the oratorio "The Seasons" was given, and later in the same year Herold gave Félicien David's "The Desert." He was leader of choruses for the Turn-Verein and the Eintracht Society. He was conductor of the Italian operas at the Metropolitan Theater. He was conductor for the San Francisco Harmonic and Händel and Haydn societies. He was the father of the only large orchestra, and he conducted performances of almost all the important orchestral works of the great composers. He instituted music festivals. If his symphonic concerts fostered culture in the classes, these festivals tended to popularize the classics with the masses.

In fact, the history of Rudolph Herold is the history of early musical progress in San Francisco. Throughout all that first, rough, pioneer period Herold incarnated pure harmony amidst the unceasing mad rush for gold.

Herold also put on for the first time in this city, with Anna Bishop as the principal singer, the oratorios "The Creation" and "Stabat Mater," and Meyerbeer's opera "Robert the Devil." He gave the opera for eight nights running. This would be an ambitious undertaking at any time; considering that San Francisco but a few years before had been only a trading station, it was a colossal achievement.

Madame Bishop was the wife of Sir Henry Bishop, the composer, who had set to music the words of "Home Sweet Home." She was accompanied to the Pacific Coast by the mountainous and stooping Robert Bochsa, called the "Father of the Harp," for whom, it was said, she had deserted her husband.

Madame Bishop, already known in all the principal cities of Europe and in the Eastern States, arrived in San Francisco in February, 1854. With fewer original good notes than any of the singers who had as yet come to the West, she was nevertheless an experienced singer, with notes pure, clear, round, and ringing, and with great powers of vocal endurance. She remained upwards of two years, returned on a concert tour in 1864, and for the last time in 1873. On her pioneer tour she gave California its first experience of the operas "Don Pasquale," "Linda," "Lucrezia Borgia," "Fra Diavolo," "Martha," and "Der Freischütz." In the second act of "Der Freischütz" the gas went out, and the audience had to leave.

But, triumphing over all obstacles, by the fall of 1854 Herold had established classical music in San Francisco.

# 22

## Lola Montez

LOLA MONTEZ, the world-renowned dancer, who appeared on the San Francisco stage in the early 'fifties, was a woman like a glorious sun that sinks into a black night. Had her love of power extended to sovereignty over herself, had her summary chastisement of others been balanced by an occasional chastisement of self, her days might have been all radiance. But she knew no self-discipline: so the world disciplined her. She was once the mistress and favorite of a king, and she ended in poverty and obscurity. A dispatch from St. Louis, dated January 22d, 1861, told San Franciscans that she had died in New York on the 17th.

Some say she died of consumption; others, of paralysis. Some say she died in a hospital; others, among them Walter Leman, a pioneer actor who had personal acquaintance with her when both appeared at the same time upon the stage of this city, that she died in a second-class boarding-house in New York City. Some say she was forty-three when she died; others, thirty-seven, holding, in this, to her own statement that 1824, and not 1818, was the year of her birth. In the memoirs of Walter Leman we find her "Countess of Landsfeldt, Baroness of the Order of St. Theresa, and discarded wife of a king, whose life-dream flickered out in obscurity, and who now lies in Trinity church yard in an humble grave, above which is the inscription, 'Elizabeth Gilbert, died in New York, aged forty-one years.' "

Lola Montez combined in her single person the qualities of many women. She was slim and petite, scarce five feet tall, yet with the imperial bearing of a Juno; so I am told by August Wetterman, who was conductor of the orchestra at the time of her appearance in San Francisco. Her hair was golden, of the North; her eyes, dark and slumbrous, of the South. She was Venus and Minerva—rare beauty, grace, and sinuosity, combined with rare intellectual powers. She was bold as a swashbuckler, courageous as a soldier, artful in address as a political intriguer, yet with a heart open and tender, capable at times of great and noble generosity. She was reckless as the wind tearing through space, willful as a colt being broken to the bridle, yet loving all the restraints that culture brings.

And even as she combined within herself the qualities, so she lived the lives, of many women. She was a woman of many loves, of marriages and several divorces, of many adventures, of virtues and follies.

At fourteen she became the wife of a Captain James, an officer in the British army, who was stationed in India. She was the wife of George Trafford Heald, a guardsman in London. She was the wife of Patrick Purdy Hull, editor of *Town Talk,* a San Francisco weekly. She was the wife—some say the mistress only—of an officer of the German army who lived for a time in Sacramento. She was "almost married," as she herself said, to the Polish prince Sulkowski, but broke off the engagement when she found that he had need of other loves besides. She was the mistress of Dujarier, a proprietor of the Paris newspaper, *La Presse,* who was killed in a duel. She was the mistress of King Ludwig of Bavaria.

Of her origin, Lola Montez asserted that she was of Irish nobility on her father's side, since he was the son of Sir Edward Gilbert, and Moorish-Spanish on her mother's side, of the noble family of the Montalvos, who were originally of Moorish blood and who came into Spain at the time of Ferdinand and Isabella. The names given her in baptism were Marie Dolores Eliza Rosanna. She was always called Dolores, the diminutive of which is Lola.

In temperament, Lola Montez was spontaneously Latin. She was likewise of the strong, independent nature that is incapable of being bound by any conventions unless they find sanction within oneself. So it came to pass that this petted favorite of a king, this personal acquaintance of Georges Sand, of Dumas *père,* of Victor Hugo, Méry, Lamartine, and Liszt, found herself eventually in California, shunned and oppressed by the women and more or less exploited by the men. In Grass Valley, where she lived for quite a while, the women attempted to burn her cabin.

The men entertained the idea of Lola Montez with broad wink and uplifted eyebrow. Even such men as Steve Massett, prince of Bohemians, and Walter Leman, fellow artist, write somewhat slurringly of her. Though one of them is willing to admit having gone to her wedding, and the other to her house party, yet in their disguising of names by the use of initials and abbreviations they both seem doubtful of the propriety of implicating others.

"At sunrise," relates Walter Leman of Lola Montez' marriage to Patrick Purdy Hull, on July 2d, 1853, "near the old Mission Church, fifteen or twenty persons were walking listlessly around, as if waiting for something; among them Governor W. and his wife, the only lady, besides the bride, who was present at the wedding.

"Presently the carriage containing Lola and Hull drove up. Lola turned, and on entering the church waved her hand to close the front door; but some forty spectators in all had already got inside.

"Lola carried in her hand two vases containing artificial white roses, and presented them to the officiating clergyman at the altar. From the church the party went to an anteroom, where there was a spread of cake, wine, cigars and cigarettes. Gov. W., giving Mr. C. a significant wink, approaching Lola kissed her, and C., to 'make the occasion memorable,' as he said, did the same. Lola made no objection, remarking, 'Such is the custom of my country.' She received the congratulations of all who were present and had a pleasant word for all; she then inquired, 'Where can we get a good breakfast?' Hull replied, 'At the Bull's Head'; Lola said she had rather go to the Tivoli; and to the Tivoli they went."

Steve Massett wrote, in 1855:

"At Grass Valley the late Mme. Lola Montez was residing in a very picturesque little villa, guarded by a large-sized bear, sundry dogs, parrots, cats, etc. She and Johnny S. received me very hospitably, and the evening with the Countesse Landsfeld and the merry groups there and then assembled—among them were Gus S. of this city and Gil M. of Baltimore—will ever be remembered by me with pleasure."

There were no great political issues to give play to her peculiar qualities of intellect. Little credence is to be placed in the rather fanciful tale that she was to be made Empress of California in return for her services in the Southern intrigues to carry the State out of the Union.

In her art, such as it was, there was play for neither intellect nor imagination. The public wanted nothing of her art except what pandered to its lowest feelings. Let the critics rave—as they did—of her graceful and impressive pantomime in "Yelva," relating in dumb show "a more thrilling scene of suffering than perhaps language could express"; let them rave of her "peculiar earnestness of manner and utterance, her depth of feeling and power to display the passions of ardent and high-souled woman"; let them recount their "surprise and pleasure" in the execution of her sailor's hornpipe, her "fresh, novel, eccentric, brilliant dancing"; the public wanted only her "spider dance" and the Bavarian drama which was supposed to depict, more or less, her doubtful connections with King Ludwig. As presented in San Francisco, the spider dance was a kind of afterpiece to the play.

Lola Montez' spider dance was world-famed. She had danced it at the courts and capitals of Europe. Her "spiders" were constructed of cork and whalebone, attached, for spring, by rubber. As they swarmed about her, in her terror she lifted her tarletan skirts ever higher about her, and the dance ended in wild abandon—or rather, in what the term signified for that day; I am told by August Wetterman, now the only surviving witness, that this highly suggestive dance of the 'fifties would seem tame today.

Here is the only description of it that I have been able to discover:

" 'Lola Montez in Bavaria' was repeated last evening, the Countess impersonating herself. The play has some interest from the historical point of view, but, asking pardon of her Countess-ship, we think it rather prosy.... But the spider dance inspired us with new life. Up went the curtain and on came Lola, fermenting the pit, agitating the gallery and sensationalizing the dress circle....

"Lola comes in—sails in—flies in—arrayed in a costume to which Joseph's coat could never think of comparing. She stands an instant, full of fire, action and abandon.

"One is reminded at first glance of a full-blooded Arabian, eloquent with force and freedom, and 'all-a-jump' with the excitement of the coming dance. Lola apparently represents a country girl in some flowery mead. She unwittingly gets into one of those huge nests of spiders, found during the springtime in the meadows, with a long radius of leading spires and fibres stretching away into an infinity of space. She commences to dance, and the cobwebs entangle her ankles. The myriad spiders, young, old and half grown, begin to colonize....

"The music, a slow-measured but fascinating amalgamation of polka, waltz, march, mazurka and jig, conforms admirably to the step. The spiders accumulate, and the danseuse stamps. They appear in myriads—eleven-legged nondescripts with two heads and no eyes; hairy monsters with fire-clawed feelers and nimble shanks.

"They crawl and sprattle about the stage, invading the fringes of Miladi's petticoats and taking such unwarrantable liberties that the spectator imagines an inextricable mass of cobwebs and enraged spiders, and would sympathize with the demoiselle, but she seems to take it so easily herself that one quickly jumps to the conclusion that she is enough for them. It is Lola versus the spiders.

"After a series of examinations and shaking of dresses, she succeeds in getting the imaginary intruders away—apparently stamps daylight out of the last of the ten thousand, and does it with so much naïveté that we feel a sort of satisfaction at the triumph.

"The picture winds up with Lola's victory, and she glides from the stage overwhelmed with applause, and smashed spiders, and radiant with parti-colored skirts, smiles, graces, cobwebs and glory."

Immediately after Lola Montez' departure for the interior, Caroline Chapman gave, in "Spy-dear," upon the boards of San Francisco Hall, a burlesque of Lola Montez' spider dance, which jammed the theater nightly and was the gossip, for weeks, of the Ambrosial Path.

Previous to her departure, Lola Montez had been called upon to give her services at a benefit performance for the firemen's fund. Through her unusual executive ability, Lola Montez had contributed more than any other one person to its success, in the unprecedented number of stars she had gathered together for the event.

One citizen, at least, was found to reprove Miss Chapman's burlesque of Lola, in an open letter, dated June 26th, 1853, which is given herewith:

Editor of the Herald: Curiosity to witness for a second time the new local burlesque attracted me to the San Francisco Theatre last evening. I happened to be present at its first presentation, when, taken by surprise by the novelty of its features, and carried completely away by the drollery of the principal performers, I laughed with the loudest and abandoned myself to the enjoyment of the moment, without thinking or caring much about the object or effect of the piece.

A second representation has produced other and very different sensations. With the exception of Miss Chapman's bravura, and Mr. Chapman's grotesque dance, which after all are the great points in the burlesque, but which would be equally amusing if entirely disconnected with it, the whole affair is an exceedingly coarse and vulgar attack upon one who, whatever her faults or foibles may have been, has proved herself a noble-hearted and generous woman, and who little deserves that her exertions in behalf of suffering humanity, so freely offered [Lola Montez performed for firemen's benefits], so readily accepted, should be repaid by ridicule and scurrility.

Who is there that, after serious reflection on the character and conduct of Lola Montez while a visitor among us, can go and witness with pleasure and delight a vulgar misrepresentation of her manners and behavior, a ridiculous caricature of her person and a coarse exaggeration of her peculiarities? Not you, gallant firemen of San Francisco, of whom she spoke with so much heartfelt enthusiasm, and to whose noble charity she so freely and voluntarily contributed thousands of dollars. Not you, members of the Benevolent Association, for whom she toiled with so much pleasure, well knowing that the widespread reach of your charity was not confined by prejudice of race or religion—not you, or those who through you have become grateful recipients of her bounty. Not anyone who possesses a particle of taste, a spark of chivalry, or a feeling of sympathy for an unprotected but lovely, generous and confiding woman, in his composition.

Mr. Chapman's personation of Baker, and Mr. Dumfries' of Thomas, are less exceptionable, and are really exceedingly droll and mirth-exciting performances. The gentlemen represented probably care little about the matter, unless, as giving them a little extra notoriety, they find it rather gratifying than otherwise; if, on the contrary, they dislike it, they can turn the tables on their caricaturists, by acting them (how I should like to see Baker try his hand at Billy Chapman), and thus they have their remedy.

Such performances as the "Spy-dear Dance," though sufficiently nonsensical, are at any rate legitimate sources of fun, and occasionally exceedingly amusing. But a lady!—gentlemen—a lady! If no gratitude is felt for her benevolence, good taste should have decreed at least that her name and character should not be publicly ridiculed and outraged in this community.

But besides all this, there is another stringent reason why this effort of genius should not have been placed before the public. There probably never was, and never will be, an actress in San Francisco who has made more warm friends and admirers than Miss Caroline Chapman. She can play anything and everything, and do it well, and her name is an unfailing source of attraction wherever she appears. No matter what she undertakes, she renders herself acceptable, and generally far more than acceptable, to her audience. If she were to "play the Devil," I haven't the least doubt she would do it perfectly, and be greeted with roars of applause; *but we don't want to see her in any such character.*

Miss Chapman is a lady, and a most admirable artist, and I cannot believe that lowering her in this manner to a more profound depth than I had supposed low comedy to be capable of can be any more agreeable to herself than it is to her admirers.

"It's really not at all in her way." No! no! we've had enough of this; personalities may amuse for a moment, but a little reflection makes them offensive. Give us "BEAUTY" again, charming Carry, and don't let them make a *Mule* of you any longer.

S.

At Sacramento, Lola Montez proved quite capable of defending herself. Someone had laughed in the midst of her spider dance. Grown suspicious of men, and sensitive, she refused to go on. The next night it was said that she "came off victor amid great applause." The editor of one of the Sacramento papers, however, declared it sham applause and protested that the house had been "papered" with her friends:

"The house might be called full, but in looking it over we could distinguish only a few, a very few, of our citizens present. To strangers, impelled by mere curiosity, and the free use of free tickets is she indebted for an audience."

This is what she replied:

To the Responsible Editor of the Daily California—Sir:

The extraordinary article concerning myself which appeared in your paper this morning requires an extraordinary answer. I use the word "extraordinary," for I am astonished that a "respectable" editor should lie in such a barefaced manner and be so void of gallantry and courtesy as yourself. I am a woman. I do not advocate woman's rights, but at the same time I can right myself by inflicting summary justice upon all jack-a-napes!!! After such a gross insult you must don petticoats. I have brought some with me which I can lend for the occasion. You must fight with me. I leave the choice of weapons to yourself, for I am very magnanimous. You may choose between my dueling pistols or take your choice of a pill out of a pill box. One shall be poison and the other not, and the chances are even. I request that this affair may be arranged by your seconds as soon as possible, as my time is quite as valuable as your own.

Marie de Landsfeld Hull
(Lola Montes)

It was not long, however, in this hostile atmosphere, with little for her head and nothing for her heart, that her will, like her health, was to become broken.

In 1855 she returned to San Francisco to set sail for Australia. The night before her departure, Walter Leman, together with Laura Keene, the leading lady, and others of the company playing at the American Theater, went to her lodgings at the International Hotel, "to drink a glass of wine and to say good-bye."

"I think," says Walter Leman, in writing of this occasion, "that she had begun to abate something of the imperious and reckless manner for which she had been notorious."

# 23

# Adah Isaacs Menken

ADAH ISAACS MENKEN was a Bird of Paradise, much as was Lola Montez, and she possessed, like her, unusual intellect, a great heart, and great physical beauty. Like Lola Montez, too, she drew about her the great ones of her day. Swinburne was her friend, Dumas *père,* Joaquin Miller, Dickens.

"Books, a shelf-load of books," declared Joaquin Miller, "could not hold half that has been written on this Jewish woman's beauty of form. And beautiful she was in form; but to me her fascination lay in her beauty of mind, her soul and sweet sympathy, her sensibility to all that was beautiful in form, color, life, heart, humanity. Her face resembled, in a feminine way of course, the pictures of Lord Byron, and she wore her hair and arranged her throat so as to heighten this resemblance. Like Lord Byron, she was always trying to make believe she was dreadfully bad; that is, in her intercourse with the world about her. But in her soul she was very much another woman. She was sincere there, earnest, sad, piteously sad, though her outer life, as all know who came near her, was one continuous ripple of laughter."

Like Lola Montez, "The Menken," as she was usually called, was many times married and divorced. She boasted, however, that whereas "Lola Montez had begun with kings and ended with cowboys," she herself had "begun with cowboys and ended with kings." But again like Lola Montez, she could not wholly withdraw herself from men who sought to devour her mere physical loveliness, nor could she subdue and unify the warring elements of her many-sided nature.

In the characteristic language of Joaquin Miller, "little is known of her except lies." Some say she was born in New Orleans, and that she embraced the Jewish faith upon her mother's marriage to a Jew; others, that she received her name upon her own marriage to the Jewish merchant, Alexander Isaacs Menken, whose name she retained to her death. Joaquin Miller gives her birthplace as Cincinnati, Ohio, and says she was born of Jewish parents, who migrated to New Orleans when she was a child. There, in her twenty-first year, she met Menken, who was wont to come to New Orleans as his principal trading station.

She married Menken in 1856. She married John C. Heenan, the prize fighter, known as the "Benicia Boy," in 1859. Divorced from him, she became, in 1862, the wife of Robert Newell, known to the literary world as Orpheus C. Kerr. Divorced from him in 1865, she became in 1866 the wife of James Barclay.

Newell, as Orpheus C. Kerr, gave her world fame as the "equestrian actress" in the play, "Mazeppa; or, the Wild Horse of Tartary." Until her death, despite the divorce, he remained ever her loyal friend. She first met Newell in 1860, in New York, where she wrote poems for the *Sunday Mercury* and numerous prose articles for *Table Talk,* of which, under his pseudonym, he was the editor.

Adah Isaacs Menken was poetess, actress, dancer. She had studied sculpture in Ohio. She had made her debut as dancer in the French Opera House in New Orleans, and had danced with such success in Havana that the Cubans called her "The Queen of the Plaza." As a dancer she had won the hearts of the people of Mexico. She had written literary criticism for newspapers in New Orleans and had published a little volume of poems, called *Memories.*

Mortified, in the city of New York, at not being able to support herself by her pen, always the cherished desire of her heart, she became a dancer in one of the concert halls on Broadway. "The poorest weapon a woman can wield is her pen," she declared. The next that was heard of her, she had set the entire West ablaze with "Mazeppa," which, in San Francisco, opened at Maguire's Opera House on August 24th, 1863. Her performance became the sensation of two continents and won for her, in a few short months, fortune and renown as "the woman with the world-famous shape."

"Mazeppa" is a love story, the play being an adaptation of Byron's poem. The climax hinges on the infliction of the Tartars' death penalty upon the hero, and The Menken took the part of the hero. The Tartars execute sentence of death by stripping the offender of his clothing and lashing him hand and foot to a wild horse, which is then headed in the direction of its native mountains and let go.

Only the equestrian skill of Mazeppa saves him. With his elbows and knees he controls and directs his wild steed to safety. Disguised as a warrior, he returns, and in a grand passage at arms vanquishes his enemies and wins love and happiness.

Whether "Mazeppa" had been essayed in a minor way in the East, I am unable to say. But the record shows that Adah Isaacs Menken's success as an equestrian actress was first made in the West. Her first-night performance put a clean $1640 in Tom Maguire's pocket. She continued to play at Maguire's and in the inland towns until April, 1864. It was in this engagement that she set the style in spit curls which the men followed—a style which enabled Johnny Carroll, as you remember, to be the sensation of the ball given by High-toned Twelve with his initials, "J. C. C.," plastered on his forehead by the deft hand of Johnny, the barber. The men "went crazy about The Menken," so Johnny informed me, and used to block the sidewalk in front of her hotel and line the streets in front of the theater to catch a glimpse of her.

Of the first performance in this city, a San Francisco critic had this to say:

"At an early hour last evening Washington Street and all the adjacent thoroughfares were thronged with people, all intent on effecting the most desirable position, in fact, any position, in Maguire's Opera House, to assist at the initial performance of Adah Isaacs Menken in 'Mazeppa.' We doubt if a similar audience was ever gathered on like occasion. Dress circle and parquet were radiant with female beauty and in point of character the assemblage was brilliant in the extreme. . . . Aside from her personal attractions, which are great, . . . she is all grace, a model for the sculptor and painter, every action being the poetry of motion.

"As a warrior she dealt blows with more muscular strength than is generally exhibited on the stage, and her horseback exercise is immense. She vaults the back of the 'fiery and untamed steed,' represented by a full-blooded California mustang, with all the daring and aplomb of a Sebastian or a Franconi, carrying the house by storm, clad in nothing but flesh-colored tights, with hair streaming down her back, and both horse and rider made the aerial flight with due precision and effect. The steed fairly galloped over the mountains of Tartary, appearing and reappearing in the distance until horse and rider were lost to view."

Throughout this engagement The Menken was assisted by Maguire's stock company—Junius Brutus Booth, Frank Mayo, Sophie Edwin, and David Anderson. Joaquin Miller, from his personal observation, tells of their attitude toward her:

"I had a friend, Pres Dean, who was then bringing out Lotta at a little place called Gilbert's Melodeon, on Portsmouth Square, and as I was with him much, and doing some smaller work only, I was enabled to be behind the scenes much at most theatres.

"Such confusion at rehearsal never was seen as when she brought on her horse and tried to tame that mean mob of actors at Maguire's to something like discipline. Booth was there, 'June' Booth, and he, it seems, should have stood by and tried to help her with his moral influence over the mob. But he did not; only sneered with the rest; and day after day kept prophesying failure and dire disgrace. And so the poor little woman had to carry the whole load of 'forty thieves' on her thin little shoulders.

"On one occasion the man who was hacking swords with Booth let the iron slip from his hand and it went whirling past Booth's head. Then Booth threw down his big, broad knife, and, rushing up and down the stage, simply roared. He disappeared then, vowing he would never, never return, and Menken after him, and I holding the horse, which some fool super in the excitement had turned loose to roam about and browse or burn his nose on the footlights. You see, I was just down out of the saddle from a year's work as express rider, and so could do almost anything with a horse. This, of course, made her tolerate me at all times, and a day or so before the great evening of opening, her first great engagement, she took me with her out to Seal Rocks, to hold her horse, mind you—nothing more than that. And I am proud to have even done that much for Adah Isaacs Menken, for she did so much for me.

"The road was all sand then—tossing, terrible, moving mountains of sand. At one place a little mountain had thrown itself right in the road before us. Our horses plunged in and wallowed belly deep, and she shouted with delight.

"She seemed very happy, half wild, all the way till we got down to the great beach beyond the Cliff House. But there, throwing herself from the saddle, she fell with her face almost in the ocean and sobbed and cried as if her heart was broken. Soon she got up, however, and, turning to where I stood holding the horse, said, smiling through her tears, 'I had to do it. They are killing me at that old playhouse, and I had to come out here and cry or die.'

"When about to remount, she ran back as a wave came in, and, throwing her tear-wet handkerchief out and cutting the gray surf, she cried: 'Good-bye, gray old grandfather, good-bye.' In fact, all her talk, dress, action, was vivid with color. Who of those days does not remember that graceful, yellow figure on the streets of San Francisco—in a single garment of yellow silk? I doubt if any other woman in the world could wear a dress like that in the winds of San Francisco and not look ludicrous. Once when calling on her and her husband at the hotel, I found her lying on a yellow skin, robed in a yellow piece of silk, and lying down flat, with her head to the fire, like an Indian."

On April 22d, 1864, she set sail from San Francisco for England. In London she created a furor even greater than here. She was the wonder and the admiration of Regent Street as she drove each day in her carriage, paneled in gold, with England's lion rampant, and drawn by a high-stepping black horse. Her dressing rooms, three in number, with piano, baths, and velvet carpets, where she gave great dinners after the evening's performance, drew daily profuse descriptions from the press."

She entered Paris in a blaze of splendor. Napoleon III attended her performance. She drove through the streets in a carriage drawn by a span of horses, the plates and buckles copper-studded, a bright yellow harness, and on the traces a hundred red tassels. Here she was even more gay, thoughtless, and convivial. Intellectual and handsome, she drew great men about her. Hospitable to a fault, she drew likewise a horde of parasites, who drained her wines and brandies, borrowed her money, and abused her. She was said to toss off brandy "with the gluttony of a hostler." The cigarette ashes were never lacking, spilled on the white tunic she habitually wore. Her name was bandied about by the gossips with that of Dumas *père*. She was said to be the slave of her passions. It was as if, after she had capitalized her physical loveliness, her equally lovely soul sorrowfully withdrew and let the body, in its arrogance of dominion, destroy itself.

One day, having returned to London to play at a benefit (like Lola Montez, she was always doing something for somebody in distress), in a fall from her horse she sustained an internal injury. She played no more; but the extravagances continued. The sheriff took her horses, carriages, and jewels. She was thrown into jail for debt. Her health, undermined by her injury and her indiscretions, became still more impaired by the wretched state of the jail. Upon obtaining her release, she returned to Paris. And there she died, it is said, of "the abuse of alcohol and ... indulgence in imperative exercise."

She was fearful of death. From the beginning she insisted that the injury from her fall would prove fatal. She had been seized with a strange chill, which she interpreted as death's touch. In her last days she persisted in having her pet dog in bed with her. When chided, she declared her belief that dogs invariably desert the dying and so long as the pet was content to remain with her she knew her time had not yet come.

She died in the Jewish faith, on Monday, August 10th, 1868, in the thirty-third year of her age, in the Rue Crématine. She was temporarily buried in Père la Chaise. In April of the next year the remains were removed to their final resting place in Montparnasse.

She died alone. Friends and parasites had fallen away when her money was gone. Only twelve persons attended her funeral. Half of these were tradesmen and servants; the rest, actors from the theater where she had played.

Shortly before her death, *Infelicia,* a book of her poems, written for the most part in San Francisco, and dedicated to Charles Dickens, was published in London. Of this book Joaquin Miller spoke highly.

"If you care for poetry, grand, sublime, majestic, get this one little book of Adah Isaacs Menken and read it from lid to lid. It is the best that America has yet to offer in the line of sublime thought. You will bear me witness that I never criticize or commend books, or mention them at all as a rule. There are better things than books for a man who can afford to live in the woods as I do. And so I have not one book in the world, except the Bible. But if I did not know this little book of hers by heart I would surely buy it."

On the flyleaf is inscribed this introductory verse:

> Leaves pallid and somber and ruddy,
>    Dead fruits of the fugitive years,
> Some stained as with wine and made bloody,
>    And some as with tears.

# 24

# Matilda Heron

IN THE PERIOD of thc 'fiftics, whatever despair might fill the hearts of men on the steamers outbound from San Francisco, on the inbound vessels people's hearts were filled with hope—hope of gold to be found in the mines, of fortunes to be made in this land of opportunity. But from an inbound steamer, on Christmas Day, 1853, Matilda Heron, a young actress of twenty-three years, stepped upon the dock in this land of promise with a heart full of despair. She had set out from the East in the rush which followed Biscaccianti's discovery that San Francisco was the "actor's El Dorado." She had been upon the stage two years. She had made no sensation, yet was regarded as an actress of ability. She was a pupil of Peter Richings, an exponent of the ultra-quiet school of acting at a period when ranting and elocution were the accepted means of portraying intense or heroic emotions.

Young, ambitious, confident of success in a young country untrammeled by tradition, Matilda Heron had set sail under the protection of her agent, Mr. George Lewis, a man well known to the profession. He became ill on the voyage and died six days before the arrival of the steamer.

Depressed by the death of her agent, alone, friendless, and doubtful of obtaining, unheralded, any engagement in this remote frontier town, she was on the point of returning home by the next steamer when fate willed otherwise. It so happened that in Boston she had played in the company of James E. Murdoch, the noted tragedian; and he, too, was at this time in San Francisco. After playing a prolonged engagement at the American, he had gone over to the new theater, the Metropolitan, where, on Christmas Eve, before a brilliant audience, he had appeared as the star attraction. The American, lacking a counter-attraction, had been compelled temporarily to close its doors.

Murdoch, on being told of the young actress' presence and her plight, hastened to the rescue. Through his endorsement of her as an actress of ability, he succeeded in gaining for her a brief engagement at the American. Moreover, her youth, her beauty, and her friendlessness aroused all the chivalry in the men of the city; they organized to insure her a full house.

On December 26th, when she opened as Bianca, the Italian wife, in Dr. Millman's play, "Fazio," she was greeted by an audience which packed the theater to the doors. She won more than half of them before she uttered a line, and long before the play was over she had captured the entire house. Her acting, simple yet intense, emotional without rant, held them spellbound. There were more men than women in the audience, yet never had there been so many tear-filled eyes. So insistent were the curtain calls for the actress, so deafening the applause, that finally, flushed with triumph, timid though happy, she stepped forward and, amid a shower of bouquets, addressed them:

"Ladies and Gentlemen: For the first time in my life I raise my voice on this side of the curtain. Totally unprepared to speak, I assure you from my heart I thank you for your kindly welcome of a poor, friendless stranger to your shores."

The critics the next day one and all declared that this "her first appearance was the greatest triumph ever achieved upon the stage in California."

"Her conception of the character of Bianca," declared the *Herald,* "is faultless, and throughout the piece her acting bore the impress of genius of no ordinary standard. The part of Bianca is one to test the intellectual and physical powers of an actress. For its natural and forceful impersonation are required histrionic powers of the highest order, and there is nothing in the range of drama which affords a severer trial to the merits of a candidate for professional fame. That Miss Heron, on her first appearance, playing to a strange audience and in a strange theatre, to which her voice is unused, should have elicited from the audience demonstrations of unqualified delight, furnished triumphant evidence of her possession of rare talent and the admirable training by which that talent has been turned to account. Should she continue to pursue a profession for which she seems to have a great fondness, it is easy to predict that she will be, in a short time, second to none on the American stage."

Even as the pioneer dramatic critic of the *Daily Alta California,* Ferdinand C. Ewer, was prophetic in his judgment of the budding genius of Edwin Booth, so the *Herald* was prophetic in its praise of Miss Heron. The world was indebted to San Francisco for her discovery, and in a few short years she was to be known as the most famous American Camille. No other actress had the power to make so many "great, strong, hard, middle-aged men weep over her Camille." From her English version of the play by Dumas *fils* she realized a fortune.

Miss Heron was not the original American Camille: Mrs. Jean Davenport-Lander had that distinction; but her version was an expurgated adaptation from the French play, and her Camille was the English rather than the French courtesan. This version San Francisco was the first to witness, when Jean Davenport played it here in 1855, with Charles Wheatleigh, of "Under the Gaslight" fame, as Armand in the first performance, and young Edwin Booth in that character in the second. Sarah Bernhardt, later seen here in a famous "Camille," spoke in French.

But if Miss Heron was not the original American Camille, it was her version of the play that was to be accepted as the standard American version of her time, and it has been used by a long list of English-speaking Camilles that have followed her, including Clara Morris, Modjeska, Lucille

Western, Alice Lingard, Nance O'Neill, Rose Coghlan, Marie Wainwright, Fanny Davenport, and Olga Nethersole.

Miss Heron was inspired to attempt the part after seeing in Paris the performance of Madame Doche, the original Camille. The younger Dumas had interested Charles Fechter, the actor, in the role of Armand, but the play had gone begging for a Camille until it finally reached Madame Doche, who made an instant success upon her first presentation of it on February 2d, 1852, at the Vaudeville. Miss Heron, who was a writer as well as an actress, and a contributor to periodicals and newspapers, on her return home after seeing Madame Doche's performance, set to work immediately on an English version, which she completed in a month's time.

This version she tried out in Cincinnati, St. Louis, and other towns while on a starring tour in 1856 and 1857, but without any success. Finally, she won over the management of Wallack's Lyceum Theater in New York, where, despite predictions that she would make a fiasco of the part, she opened in "Camille" on the evening of January 22d, 1857. Three days before the performance, E. A. Sothern was suddenly called upon to take the role of Armand. To the surprise and amazement of everyone he declared himself completely ready, and showed up next morning at rehearsal letter perfect.

There was a violent snowstorm on the opening night, and the play opened to half a house, which proved, however, to be an audience of discernment. Miss Heron's Camille was a triumph, and Mr. Sothern, for the first time, received enthusiastic calls—the beginning of a career that was to be world-famous. The play ran for forty-five nights, and closed to a crowded house.

The American, which had been wholly eclipsed by the opening of the new theater, the Metropolitan, now, in turn, through the sudden advent of this young, strange actress, entirely eclipsed the Metropolitan. A crowded house greeted Miss Heron's next night's performance of Knowles' "Love."

On December 31st, Miss Heron gave a benefit performance of "The Lady of Lyons," the proceeds of which she gave to the widow of her agent, Mr. Lewis. She played the part of Pauline.

"There have been a great many representations of Pauline in 'The Lady of Lyons,' in San Francisco, within the last two years," declared the critics next day. "At least, attempts at it have been made, but though others have done well in it, there has never been one who deserved to be placed in comparison with Miss Heron. She so far exceeds them all it appears impossible it is the same character. It is needless to enter into details of Miss Heron's acting. It is needless to notice her at all. She has got such a hold on the good nature of our people that she can defy the critics. Her acting is true to nature. She shows the woman in all her grace and loveliness, and she moves the hearts of her audience as actress never did before in California."

At the close of this performance, the audience applauded thunderously for her appearance. Mr. Baker, one of the management, who had played Fazio to her Bianca on the opening night, led her before the curtain. In one of the parquet boxes a spectator arose and handed Baker a note and a bouquet in which was hidden a jewel casket. Baker opened the note and read it aloud to the audience.

"Dear Young Lady: A few among the thousands whom your merits have already made your friends in California desire to present you with this small evidence of their esteem. It is a symbol of the religion you profess, and we trust that, while it reminds you of your faith, it will, at the same time, be received as a pledge that Genius never can be friendless on our shores."

The "small evidence of esteem" was a magnificent cross of diamonds, numbering seven large brilliants, to be worn as a brooch.

Miss Heron, after some moments' hesitation, in which she betrayed surprise and agitation, advanced and spoke as follows, frequently pausing as her emotion or the applause of her audience interrupted her:

"What shall I do, ladies and gentlemen? The position of speechmaker does not belong to a lady; nor was it my intention, when led forward by Mr. Baker, to raise my voice. But I must tell you how happy you have made me. Your kindness has completely overcome me. You have, in fact, made me a child, and I cannot find language to address you as I should. I cannot speak my gratitude. This beautiful gift, rich as it is in its jewels, has yet a richer value for me—that of being the gift of kind, good and dear friends. And I value it too as the emblem of that religion which has always been my guide, my hope and my consolation. Whenever I gaze at it, however often I may otherwise think of you, it will serve to turn my thoughts to Heaven in prayer for your welfare and happiness. I can only repeat my sincere and heartfelt thanks."

A shower of bouquets fell around her. She again came forward, and retired amid a furor of applause. The people thronged the sidewalk awaiting her appearance upon the street, and escorted her carriage back to the hotel.

Matilda Heron played twelve nights at the American and then, under engagement to Mrs. Sinclair, manager of the new theater, she went over to the Metropolitan, opening on the night of February 13th, 1854. Here, with the exception of a professional tour to the interior, she remained until her departure for the East in June.

As a historical event this engagement of Matilda Heron at the Metropolitan has importance. For at the Metropolitan, Edwin Booth, then just reaching his majority, was playing in stock. San Francisco Hall having been forced to close its doors upon the opening of the new theater, Mrs. Sinclair had taken over to the Metropolitan Edwin Booth, his elder brother Junius, David Anderson, and several others, to become members of the new company. Here, during the Matilda Heron engagement, Edwin Booth played leading man to her star parts: Romeo to her Juliet, Fazio to her Bianca, and Clifford in "The Hunchback"; and at his benefit Miss Heron played Ophelia to his Hamlet.

Matilda Heron was but two years the senior of Edwin Booth, yet in this brief engagement she put the final stamp on his style of acting; at least she determined the method which was to characterize his immortal art. The faculty of the true artist to step from an important role to a lesser one had been thoroughly developed in Edwin through his long apprenticeship as utility man in his brother's stock company, and under the same taskmaster he had also been rigorously disciplined in subduing any untoward ranting or declamation by the frequent changes from tragedy to comedy. Now, for the first time, he had nightly before his eyes an exemplification of emotional power to be gained, even in the greatest tragedy parts, by the quieter style as against that of the old "windmill" school. To her influence he owed much of the greatness of his Hamlet, "delicately and justly conceived, remarkable for its sobriety but intense power of acting."

Because it shows the influence of Matilda Heron's art upon Booth's, and affords also a vivid idea of the activity of the time, I give somewhat at length the criticism of Ferdinand C. Ewer, the friend, guide, and first critic of the famous actor. At first he was inclined to withstand the enthusiasm of the other critics for Miss Heron, but as the following, from his monthly, the *Pioneer,* shows, he finally came completely under her spell:

"The *Pioneer* cannot be so extravagant in its praise of Miss Heron as some of our citizens, and they are good critics, too. For we have kept aloof from the furor raised by high admiration and warm personal feeling and do not believe the lady surpasses everyone that has been or is upon the boards. But we desire to place at least one more laurel branch in the crown that rests so gracefully and so justly upon her temples and pronounce her above all criticism, except that of the very highest character....

"Miss Heron stands in that rare region whence creations are produced. But as yet most of her work requires those last touches which only experience can enable the perfect artist to give. One cannot but admire the freedom with which she steps forth from the trammels of the past. Her general rule appears to be never to exceed nature, and it must be confessed her exceptions are few. She gives to a terrific scene its fullest effect by the intensified whisper, rather than by that species of noise that lies just this side of ranting.

"Upon the stage she moves with ease, and as a general thing, with great grace. But at times her step is too artistic. We do not object to its style, but now and then to its degree. She possesses a fine eye, and a face capable of assuming almost every shade of expression—hate, scorn, love, supplication, fear, disgust—everything but madness—if, indeed we are to judge from one instance only.... But we do not intend to criticise. It is our object merely to note briefly a few impressions.

"The variety, the appropriateness, the wealth of her gesticulations are remarkable. In grief or torture her hands are wrung in every conceivable shape, and now and then her hand will wander to her head as though by no will of her own, as though it were attracted there by some strange power, as though there was nothing realized by her but the pain of her throbbing brain. The main fault found with her by the audience is that at times she does not speak with sufficient loudness to be heard. They allude to it as though it were some important blemish in her as an actress. Of course this is folly. She will easily remedy the mistake.

"There is one point about some of her scenes—the last in 'Romeo and Juliet,' for instance—which cannot fail to strike the beholder as very fine. We speak of the perfect abandon of her movements. In the scene alluded to she seems to have forgotten everything but her grief. In the representations of other actresses one cannot fail to feel that they are well aware, at the time, of the exact position in which they are standing, kneeling or reclining. With Miss Heron it was not so. Everything was true to nature. Each position at the dead body of Romeo was appropriate, and her anguish only appeared the greater from the carelessness of her attitude. She attained the perfection of her art.

"Then again, as she drew herself toward the body of Romeo, she did not (having reached him) drop her head suddenly upon his breast, as though exhausted nature had given way before she could reach the end attained. It dropped slowly down, and having rested it there, sweetly she 'fell asleep.' Though it was in death, she had indeed reached the loved form at last and was happy. All was silent and holy. The instant when her spirit took its flight we did not know. No time was marked by her for the burst of applause. Every eye was upon her, and the audience waited through the time of the last sad breath, while the hush of death itself was upon them. The curtain fell slowly, and they still looked. The effect was tremendous, and it was a moment or two before they recovered.

"While on 'Romeo and Juliet,' we must not fail to allude to the manner in which she presented the scene when Juliet takes the sleeping potion. Most actresses approach as near to ranting in this scene as it is possible. They tear their hair and appear to be actually beating out someone's brains with the bones of their ancestors. But with Miss Heron, how different. Everything was subdued, the more frightful passages were whispered with indescribable terror. The effect was sublime and the audience breathless."

It was in this connection that Ewer, as friend and guide, took occasion to rap Booth on the knuckles of his young hand; his criticism included this reproof:

"Some of the important actors around here were not perfect in their parts. We regret to say that this remark applies with much truth to Mr. Edwin Booth. . . . Carelessness and lack of study often prove fatal to the rising hopes of a young actor. We say this with no unkindness, but with a desire to prompt Mr. Booth to a correction of these, his principal faults."

And here Ewer placed in the record concerning San Francisco that characteristic or quality for which the city is today justly famed the world over—the daring independence of its thought, even in defiance of accepted standards, and its often prophetic insight, which made it, even at that crude period, a cradle of art:

"The Californians are as good judges of acting as can be found anywhere, and they care not a fig for the opinion of New York or London. . . . If Edwin Booth played a thousand times in New York and never won a round of applause, 'What matters it?' they say. 'We have discovered in him evidence of genius and will encourage him.' . . . If Miss Heron was neglected night after night by your New York audience, if she was shoved away from the Broadway and pushed down to the Bowery or some worse stage, the San Franciscans boldly pronounce her to be among the very brightest geniuses of the age. Crowded houses follow in her train; California will lay a fortune at her feet, and wherever she may go, however she may be received in London or New York, she is always sure of a hearty welcome and a shower of bouquets from us."

At the close of Miss Heron's final performance, Chief Duane, in the name of the Fire Department, presented her a handsome gold watch, lavishly set with diamonds.

# 25

# Edwin Booth

AMONG the passengers on the steamer "California," when, ending a run from Panama, it docked at San Francisco, July 28th, 1852, was a man close to sixty, magnificent as an old Roman. His classic profile had been marred by an accident to the bridge of his nose, the years had dimmed somewhat the luster of his kindly gray eyes, and silent battles with suffering and sorrow had left their imprint of gentle melancholy and tragic determination; yet he had great beauty of countenance still, and he carried himself with the strength and grace of youth.

Beside him walked a boy of nineteen, handsome as a Greek god, with black hair, and black eyes that were large, limpid, fathomless pools, tinged with gentle melancholy. His mobile features were of the same pure, classical outline as those of the older man, and his thin body echoed the same lithe strength and grace. He carried himself with the same noble bearing, and with a gravity beyond his years.

The older man was Junius Brutus Booth, the English tragedian. The other was his young son, Edwin.

Edwin Booth, like Napoleon, had faith in his "star." Anyway, star or no star, his rise to fame was to begin in California, where awaited him that wonderful "nursery of his professional babyhood," as he himself termed it, in which he had a hard yet affectionate taskmaster in his brother Junius to drill him; a sympathctic and discerning critic, Ferdinand Ewer, to inspire him; a friend and boon companion, David Anderson, to rest and recreate his soul; and an audience spontaneous, free, and untrammeled by the accepted standards of the actor's art, to foster his originality.

The intention had been to leave young Edwin at the Booth farm in Belair, Maryland. The elder Booth had been much averse to undertaking the difficult journey to San Francisco—the tedious long sea voyage, the muleback trip across the Isthmus, the delay at Panama with the ever-present dread of tropical fever. But the importunities of his eldest son, Junius Brutus Booth, Jr., familiarly called "June" Booth, and the younger man's glowing description of the golden opportunities awaiting them in California, finally prevailed.

June Booth, with his wife, had come to San Francisco the previous year to play in stock under engagement to Thomas Maguire, owner of the second Jenny Lind Theater. June Booth was an actor of fair ability, and was noted as an athlete and "model of manly beauty." All the Booths were famed for their good looks.

A few days prior to June's arrival, however, a fire had destroyed almost the entire city, taking with it the theater. Maguire thereupon transferred his company to the Tehama Theater in Sacramento. Upon the almost immediate rehabilitation of San Francisco, June Booth was recalled to assume the duties of actor and stage manager at the third Jenny Lind Theater. In March, 1852, at his farewell benefit, upon being called before the curtain, he announced, in a brief address, his departure on the following Saturday for the Atlantic States, adding that he intended to return in July and to bring with him his illustrious father.

All the scruples of the elder Booth having been finally overcome, he had gone to New York with his son June to set sail for California. But before sailing time he was taken ill and compelled, instead, to return to his farm at Belair, and June Booth was forced to sail without him. The elder Booth recovered sufficiently to sail by the next steamer, but, still being short of a complete recovery—indeed, he was never thereafter to be left entirely unattended—he took with him Edwin, the only son yet remaining at home.

Hence it was that Edwin came to San Francisco, to make his first appearance before this western audience as Wilford, the secretary to his father's Sir Edward Mortimer, in Colman's melodrama—an admixture of serious play and music,—"The Iron Chest." The performance took place on the evening of July 30th, 1852.

The announcement that Junius Brutus Booth was to appear packed the theater. Advance notice said: "The arrival of the great tragedian will arouse and revive the drooping theatricals in this state. The name is sufficient in itself. It needs no commentary." Mere mention was made that "the younger Booth [June] and lady [his wife] have also been engaged," and not a word of the young Edwin. Yet the performance was destined to be, for Edwin, one never to be forgotten, and "The Iron Chest" was to be forever linked in his memory with all that was most stirring in his life and with his most tragic grief.

The day following the performance, which had been immediately successful, the dramatic critic of the *Alta,* Ferdinand Ewer, while descanting on the still great art of the father—"he stands among two or three at the head of his profession,"—incidentally remarked that "the great actor has grown old." Then he added, of Edwin: "Mr. E. Booth is a very judicious actor, and we shall take occasion to notice him more at length hereafter. He took the part of Wilford and was applauded throughout."

After the closing of the Jenny Lind Theater, Booth and his sons went to fill an engagement at Sacramento; but the audiences there were small and unresponsive and they soon lost what money they had made from the packed and enthusiastic houses in San Francisco. All three, father and sons, took benefits. The father, for his, played his greatest role, Richard III. "June," on the night of his benefit, essayed the role of Othello, the father playing Iago. Edwin, for his benefit, appeared as Jaffier to his father's Pierre in "Venice Preserved."

The costume of Jaffier called for somber black. That night the father, already dressed in his costume of Pierre, was idly sitting on the steps outside his dressing room. Presently Edwin approached, arrayed as Jaffier, his long black locks and his large melancholy eyes accentuating the somberness of his dress. He moved as a young lord should. The father's trained eye made a quick appraisal.

"You look like Hamlet," he exclaimed in pleased surprise. "Why do you not act Hamlet for your benefit?"

"If ever I have another," replied the boy, "I will."

This remark, so casually made, in view of the events which were rapidly to follow, was to assume for Edwin Booth the force of a vow.

Sacramento proving unprofitable, Booth and his sons returned to San Francisco to fill an engagement at the Adelphi Theater on September 30th. Booth played to a packed house, enacting another of his great characters, Sir Giles Overreach, in "A New Way to Pay Old Debts." But the Adelphi Theater, a frame structure with a pit, had little advantage over Rowe's amphitheater of canvas. And so, with no suitable theater for his plays, and the theatrical business on the whole in a bad way, the elder Booth engaged passage for the East on the "Brother Jonathan," for the following day.

On the eve of departure the father presented to his eldest son the diadem which he used in "Richard III" and which he had carried with him for years about the country, saying: "I shall never have use for it again." To Edwin he gave the greatest of all gifts—opportunity.

He had been unfit to make the outbound journey from the East to the Pacific Coast, and now, broken in health and spirit by the hardships and failure of the tour, he doubly needed someone on the long return voyage. But he would not take Edwin back. Unfit though he himself might be for this field, he saw the great advantage it offered to the novice—and Edwin had long been decided upon an actor's career. The father, using all his persuasive powers, quieted Edwin's conscience by insisting that he was fit to journey alone. And Edwin was induced to remain.

The hard times which had long threatened and which were but the beginning of the great panic of 1855 now hit San Francisco with full force. Edwin therefore accepted an offer to play alternately at Nevada City and Grass Valley—mining towns four miles apart. It was in Nevada City that he played Iago for the first time.

Both towns had a large floating population. They were the scene of the most extensive mining operations in California. For miles, like huge serpents, tunnels wound about the mountains, following the veins of gold. On all sides were immense dumps of sand and gravel thrown up from the excavations. Fertile fields of wheat and barley gaped with the wide wounds made by the miners, and the growing grain was cast ruthlessly to the waste heap in the search for the richer treasure of the earth.

The richest spot in all this region was Nevada City. It was said that there was not a foot of ground here that did not contain gold. Part of the town had been undermined by the gold diggers, so that many of the houses had to be braced by beams, and wide gulches opened in the streets. It was a town of wooden shacks, of shanty eating-houses and hotels; of unpaved, unlighted thoroughfares; built without plan, crowding into a defile in the mountains. The roar of the crushers was everywhere.

Gold, gold! Yet ruin and starvation were soon to descend. A few speculators had cornered all the flour, rice, and sugar. To add to the general misery, snow now fell for days. All travel, and all communication with the outer world, were cut off.

The theater where Edwin had been playing had been closed for a fortnight. For the little company of actors the day was near when even the meager fare that had been theirs in the days of plenty, the miserable hotel accommodations, the comfortless cot in a room with its strip of carpet, a broken water pitcher, and a single towel, would be beyond their means. On Edwin's departure from San Francisco his brother Junius had said: "Edwin, put a gold slug in the bottom of your trunk, then forget you have it. When necessity drives, take it out and use it." But Edwin Booth's fifty-dollar gold slug had long ago been unearthed from the bottom of his trunk and spent.

It was night. The dispirited boy, wondering what he should do, was groping his way through the mud and slush of the unpaved, unlighted streets, when he spied a man with a lantern coming toward him. By its faint glimmer he recognized an old actor, George Spear, familiarly known as "Old Spear." A mail carrier had finally pushed through the snow with letters from the outside world, and Old Spear, thus receiving intelligence of the death of the great tragedian, was on his way to break the news to Edwin.

"There's mail in," he said.

"What's the news?" asked the boy, eagerly; but even as he asked the question, he read the answer in the other's face.

Anguish was now added to the miseries of the young actor's lot. He had idolized his father; and he had let him depart alone. The thought tormented him, forlorn and destitute in the storm-bound wilderness.

The snow continued to fall. The actors' situation was hopeless. A group of them stood on the street corner considering their next move. "Why not walk to Marysville?"—which was fifty miles distant. The proposal, made half in jest, was taken seriously. A leader was chosen; and they went, including a violinist who was the entire orchestra of the theater.

Half starved and ill-clad, they started down the mountain to battle the endless snowdrifts. At nightfall they came to a roadside hotel, where in exchange for entertainment they could have food and shelter. Each selected from his repertory what was merriest, with which to regale the company. Edwin Booth could play the violin and strum a banjo and sing a song; he knew some Negro melodies, learned in Maryland. In spite of his grief he sang with spirit, but his youth and the sadness of his face touched the motherly heart of the hotel proprietress. She noticed how delicate he was, and that he had no overcoat. She had one that would fit him, and when he left she bustled him into it, not heeding his protests. In after years, when as a famous actor he revisited that part of California, he recalled the incident and sent his former hostess a handsome reminder.

At the end of two days the little group reached Marysville, where they dispersed.

Edwin Booth borrowed ten dollars from an acquaintance to pay his passage by steamer to Sacramento. On arriving, he found that Sacramento had been partly destroyed by fire and that almost everything that had escaped the flames had been swept away by the floods of the winter's storms. Alone and penniless, he nevertheless managed to make his way to San Francisco, where his brother Junius got him an immediate engagement to play in "The Fireman" on February 2d, 1853, at San Francisco Hall.

It was the season of the Kate Hayes engagement. On "off nights" of her concerts, Junius Booth and George Chapman rented San Francisco Hall for light plays, and it was in these that the actor-manager was able to offer Edwin parts.

At the end of Miss Hayes' season, Junius Booth, together with John Fairchild, the scenic artist, W. B. Chapman, comedian, and W. B. Hamilton, in old men's parts, took over the hall, had it renovated, changed its name to the San Francisco Theater, and opened on February 18th, with a dramatic company, in a variety of light farces and original burlesques and extravaganzas. These original productions were replete with local hits, especially in burlesques of plays and players of the rival theaters, and many of them crowded the house to overflowing. They came, for the most part, from the prolific and versatile genius of Junius Booth's next-door neighbor the druggist, Dr. Robinson, or "Yankee" Robinson, as he was often called.

June Booth lived at No. 5 Calhoun Street, on what was then called "Windmill Hill" from the windmill owned by Hudson, the tea and coffee merchant, who ground spices and coffee there. Plank sidewalks fashioned from the hulls of old ships, and an occasional flight of steps along the plank walks to counteract the steeper pitches of the grade, led to Windmill Hill from Vallejo Street. There were but few houses on the hill, which was covered for the most part with scrub oak. In the springtime it was lovely with green grass and varicolored wild flowers, and especially brilliant when the yellow blossoms flowered on the wild mustard plants growing in great abundance all about.

June Booth's house, No. 5, was next to Dr. Robinson's at No. 9, which still stands, the rise of ground having put it beyond the reach of the flames in 1906. It still bears its pioneer numbering painted crudely in white on the facade of the gateway. It is a two-story gabled frame house with a garden and trees—a palatial home for that period, when lumber was high and labor higher. The house fronts the water, and commands a grand sweep of the Bay. Booth's house was on much the same order; it has been torn down to make way for an imposing modern structure.—But this is by the way.

Of the new dramatic company under his brother's management, Edwin Booth became a member. His salary was meager, his work arduous, his position doubtful. At the opening performance he gained not so much as a mention. The reporter wrote: "Last evening, much to the gratification of the public, the San Francisco Theatre was reopened. ... The interior has been thoroughly renovated and three ventilators have been added to the dress circle, so that no discomfort can be apprehended from the absence of a full supply of fresh air. The changes of decoration, etc., have been effected with a great deal of good taste, rendering the theatre as pleasant to look upon as could be desired. All the old favorites who were wont nightly to call down roars of laughter and storms of applause from the well-filled boxes have rallied under the same successful standard, not, however, without reinforcement of a most efficient kind. Mrs. Caroline Chapman, once the life and soul of Burton's Corps Dramatique in New York, will be the center of attraction."

Edwin Booth served, in this stock company, a difficult apprenticeship. His brother cast him again and again in comedy, farce, and burlesque, and at least three times reduced him from star parts to utility; as Booth in later years remarked, "It was a lesson for crushed tragedians." For a season he played general utility to the versatile Chapman family.

Of all the Chapmans, the "bouncing" and joyous Caroline was a great favorite with the men of the 'fifties. She was an exquisite dancer and an actress of "protean ability." She seemed to perform as much for her own amusement as for that of her audience, to relish every point, and to revel in her own sprightliness. Nor did she ever seem conscious of exertion or fatigue. All this was accompanied by a dash and gracefulness with which, at one bound upon the stage, she won her audience.

The season of burlesques and extravaganzas from the versatile pen of Dr. Robinson, with Caroline Chapman and W. B. Chapman in the star parts, though a financial success for the manager, was a strenuous one for the actors. The fashion of the 'fifties was to have a play and an afterpiece. Matinees were unknown, but the evening performances lasted until past midnight, and a new play was put on almost nightly. Dr. Robinson produced them so rapidly that the players lacked time to study their parts, rehearsals were scamped, and many pieces would have failed but for the ready wit of the actors in completing on the inspiration of the moment forgotten sentences and scenes.

Audiences of the 'fifties took great delight in the burlesques of plays and players at rival houses, and in extravaganzas that were full of local hits. Here none excelled Dr. Robinson: nothing was beyond his ridicule. His "Who's Got the Countess?" took the town by storm. But his burlesque of "Hamlet" was a failure; any travesty of "Hamlet" was a sacrilege akin to a burlesque of the Scriptures.

Booth found his real opportunities, in the great tragedies, on benefit nights. The benefit, though falsely represented as a horn of plenty, in reality signaled the approach of the all-devouring locust. At benefit time, penury stalked. When the edict went forth from the box office, "Everybody go out and take a benefit," it meant that the cupboard was bare, and bare for the manager, too.

In those days the fate of the actor was inseparably bound up with that of the manager, who was far indeed from being a capitalist. More often than not he went into an enterprise on the proverbial shoestring. He rarely had sufficient financial backing to retain a theater for long leases; he rented a house for six months, or three months, or for only a single show. This precarious financial state of the manager was of vital concern to the actor, for he was wholly dependent upon the manager for theaters to play in, especially on this western coast where they were few and far between and transportation was difficult and expensive. It therefore behooved even the great star, when the manager got in a tight place, to go out and "hustle a benefit," in the hope that by helping to keep the company afloat his own salary might some day, somewhere, materialize. As a matter of fact, the benefit was only a device for getting money to pay the manager's bills. The public might rally to the glory of some shining star or the popularity of an usher or a doorkeeper, but there was little to inspire the imagination in the financial distress of a harassed business manager.

The benefit had one distinction. The lowly stage crew and the lesser lights of the company received a pro rata of the money collected on the tickets they sold. The star, on the other hand, or an actor of reputation, received a pro rata of his salary, estimated on the profits derived from the drawing power of his name.

Edwin Booth never fared well financially at benefit time. In his four years in San Francisco, with the long list of benefits which accrued to every actor, his fate in this respect may be read in the following excerpts.

"Mr. E. Booth's benefit took place last evening and we regretted to see that the house was not filled as it should have been in justice to the merits of the beneficiary, as also on account of the character of the performance."

"Mr. E. Booth, whose excellent talent as an actor is so well known to the people of San Francisco and so highly appreciated by them, took a benefit at this theatre [San Francisco Theatre] last night. The attendance, much to our regret, and we are sure, that of the public, was unaccountably small. After the overflowing houses which have attended the benefits of other performers at this theatre, who, without any disparagement to their merits, hold inferior position in the estimation of the public to that occupied by Mr. Booth, we expected to find the house crowded to its utmost capacity, and can attribute this slim attendance only to an accidental cause. On a future occasion we trust the public will have an opportunity to compensate themselves and Mr. Booth for this seeming neglect."

Not until the fall of 1856, when his farewell benefit was announced, with a possibility of his never again appearing in San Francisco—he was to sail the next day for the Atlantic States to fill a star engagement at the Broadway Theater, New York—did he enjoy a successful one, when "a brilliant audience came to pay their tribute to the genius of this young artist."

Benefit time, though, had a supreme compensation: an actor could choose to play whatever part he desired. Edwin Booth chose the great tragedies. Young as he was, he elected to enact Hamlet, Romeo, Richard III, Macbeth, Othello, and King Lear. At his first benefit, on April 22d, 1853, he essayed the role of Hamlet. The first criticism ever written on his portrayal of this character appeared in the *Daily Alta California* on April 26th:

"For the benefit of Mr. Booth, the favorite play of 'Hamlet' was produced at this establishment [San Francisco Theatre] last night, Mr. Booth supporting the principal part and making his first appearance in that difficult character. As a first appearance it may be considered highly creditable, and we can even predict a high degree of success for the promising young artist when he shall have overcome a few disagreeable faults in intonation and delivery, and reached a profounder conception of the part."

A criticism of the same impersonation made in June a year later indicates a degree of improvement:

"Mr. Booth assumed for this occasion [a benefit again] the character of Hamlet, his personation of which was observed with a deep and attentive interest. There were some defects in it, but they were generally of such a character as practice will easily remove, and there were very many points that were given with great force and called forth an earnest expression of applause. The talent which Mr. Booth possesses was frequently displayed throughout his delineation of this peculiar and arduous character, and the general excellency with which he rendered it was appropriately acknowledged."

In this performance Matilda Heron essayed the part of Ophelia, and James E. Murdoch the part of the ghost.

The following comment is from the *Daily Alta California* of June 28th, 1853, and concerns Edwin's first attempt at Romeo [at benefit time, as usual], with that joyous comedienne, Caroline Chapman, assuming the tragic role of Juliet (as on another occasion she assumed the part of the mournful Ophelia to his melancholy Dane):

"It is very seldom that a piece is put upon the stage with so strong a cast as was 'Romeo and Juliet' at the San Francisco [Theatre] last evening. It is, of course, superfluous to say anything of Miss Chapman's Juliet. The part is suited to her powers, and when that is the case it is always rendered as perfect as close study and a perfect mastery of stage effect can make it.

"The Romeo of Mr. Edwin Booth was one of the best pieces of acting of his we have ever seen. That he is a young actor of great promise there is no doubt, and that he may yet reach the highest round in his profession there is little question. But the road he has entered upon is a hard and rugged one. It requires ceaseless and lifelong effort to attain the highest rank, and it is no honest or candid pen that tells him he has already reached it. Yet the part was rendered last evening most effectually and was the best we have ever seen from him."

But never to be forgotten by Edwin Booth was the very first criticism given him, in his twentieth year, in the *Daily Alta California* of April 22d, 1853, after his performance of Richard III, on the occasion of the benefit of the scenic artist, John Fairchild. This was the first of the many criticisms of Booth's acting that were written by Ferdinand C. Ewer, who from the first was favorably impressed.

"There was a splendid house to witness the production of Shakespeare's never-failing 'Richard III' at the San Francisco [Theatre] last evening. Mr. Booth ('Young Booth,' as he is familiarly called) personated the 'bloody and devouring' Richard in a manner that betokened a just conception, and gave promise of an ability which in coming years will place his name foremost among the actors of the day."

On the day that Ewer wrote this, a lifelong friendship between the two young men began. It takes genius to discern genius. Had Ewer been less, Edwin Booth might not have been so great.

Ewer was a many-sided genius. Of all the critics in San Francisco he wielded by far the greatest influence upon early theatricals. Not only did he write dramatic criticism for the *Alta,* but also thoughtful reviews, filled with helpful suggestions and wise counsel, for the monthly *Pioneer*. Besides the *Pioneer,* he was also editor and founder of the *Daily Transcript,* and was the author, as well, of a book entitled

*Two Eventful Nights,* issued in 1856. Later he was ordained an Episcopalian clergyman.

Ewer was born in Nantucket, of Quaker parents. He entered Harvard to prepare for the ministry. Overtaken with skepticism, he changed from theology to civil engineering. Fresh from college, he sailed, in 1849, around the Horn for San Francisco, at the outbreak of the gold fever. He entered the Custom House as a clerk under Milton Latham, but continued to pursue his calling as writer and dramatic critic.

It is by virtue of Ewer's criticisms that San Francisco lays claim to the "discovery" of Edwin Booth. Sacramento has put in a counter claim, based on the remark of one of its critics that "the character of the Prince of Denmark was most vividly and truthfully portrayed by Mr. E. Booth, Saturday evening, and in some scenes his acting would compare favorably with Murdoch."

To Booth this was high praise, for Murdoch had been his teacher in elocution. To equal him had been his ambition. But Ewer wrote, in the *Pioneer:*

"The Californians are as good judges as can be found anywhere, and they care not a fig for the opinion of New York or London.

"If Murdoch comes here heralded by the laudations of the press (from Maine to Texas they say 'he is a very fair actor') they are not blind to the fact that in whatever character he appears he is always Murdoch—Murdoch—Murdoch. They give him fair houses, but prefer Stark most decidedly in 'Richelieu.' . . .

"If Edwin Booth played a thousand times in New York and never won a round of applause, 'What matters it?' they say. 'We discovered in him evidence of genius and we will encourage him, trusting that he will commence sooner or later *studying* and preparing himself by hard work for the position he is capable of attaining.'

"This is high talk," continues Ewer. "But the stamp of a San Francisco audience, of however little weight it may be among the Cockneys or the Knickerbockers, is no such small matter after all, for when we pronounce a favorable verdict we are able to back it up with a fortune and snap our fingers in the face of the world."

If Edwin owed much to Ewer for encouraging him in his profession, he owed even more to David C. Anderson for fortifying his personal character and lightening his naturally melancholy spirit.

In September, 1853, Anderson, who had been playing at the American Theater, obtained an engagement at the San Francisco Theater. He was an actor of character parts. He was the first person in California to play the ghost in "Hamlet." He came to the Pacific Coast in 1851, and began playing at the Tehama Theater in Sacramento. His Sir Peter Teazle, in "The School for Scandal," commanded the admiration of the critics. Many considered his Polonius in "Hamlet" one of the greatest in the history of the stage. He was tall and rather thin, with refined features, aristocratic bearing, and cultivated manners, and was a man of considerable scholastic attainments.

His boon companion before he met Edwin Booth had been William Barry, an eccentric low comedian who became known for his excellence as the First Gravedigger in "Hamlet." Anderson and Barry, in the reaction that so often follows upon an actor's mental and emotional concentration, would swing far to the other extreme and riot through the country on a prolonged debauch. It is related that on one such occasion they planted gold in a potato patch of a farmer's ranch in Yolo County, just outside the confines of Sacramento. Upon discovering the yellow dust, the farmer dug up all his potatoes and began to mine his ranch. Once, they encountered an expressman standing at the curb, bought his whole outfit, and took joyously to hauling trunks, charging all the traffic would bear—five dollars a trunk. People paid the fee blithely, condoning, in the spirit of the time, the failing of those they loved. Actors at that period were the idols of the people. Without a cent in their pockets, Anderson and Barry could get, at any of the bars, all the drink their thirst at such times demanded; for it was considered an attraction to have them about.

Young as Edwin Booth was, he had already begun to find that the pleasures of alcohol might be a problem. With Anderson, who had decided to mend his own ways, he took a vow to be "temperate, virtuous, and domestic." They bought a plot of ground on the Mission road and built thereon a shack with two rooms. They called the place a ranch—and as such they extravagantly registered it in the City Directory. Where was this ranch? Do you remember

"Pipesville," Steve Massett's yellow cottage in the marsh by the "bridge" on Mission Street? The "ranch" of Booth and Anderson was no more than five hundred feet beyond.

"We had a horse and wagon," Edwin relates, "and we drove into town to get provisions. Kidneys were cheap and we bought them whenever we could."

The two friends worked and "ranched" happily together till the theater succumbed to hard times in the spring of 1854 and set them to hunting for more profitable fields of endeavor.

We have, however, run a little ahead of our story. The San Francisco Theater, it will be remembered, in the summer of 1853 had begun to decline. "June" Booth, the manager, ordered everybody to take benetfis—Dr. Robinson, Edwin Booth, Caroline Chapman, the doorkeeper, the usher—but it was all to no avail. By September it was announced that Trench the architect was putting up a new playhouse, the Metropolitan, just around the corner on Montgomery Street, for Mrs. Sinclair, the wife of Edwin Forrest. She was herself to be the manager, and in the interim she had taken a temporary lease of San Francisco Hall.

On Christmas Eve the new theater was opened. The old one was turned into a theater for Negro minstrelsy, and did not regain its former splendor until several years later, when, remodeled beyond recognition, it was opened as Maguire's Opera House. Junius Booth was engaged as stage manager for the new theater, and Edwin Booth and David Anderson as stock actors.

The Metropolitan Theater was announced as "the handsomest temple of the dramatic art in America." The opening night was brilliantly attended, with James E. Murdoch, the tragedian, as star. Mrs. Sinclair, in a curtain speech, announced her plans to conduct the theater on an unprecedented scale, which met with tremendous applause.

"I have engaged Mr. Murdoch," she said, "as first star for a dramatic season. (Great applause.) I have made arrangements to produce a series of English Opera with Madame Anna Thillon (applause), and this distinguished artist will shortly have the honor of appearing before you. Montplaisir and the French ballet troupe will appear immediately on these boards (applause)."

No mention, this opening night, was made of the engagement of Edwin Booth. The next day, for the off night, a line appeared stating that Edwin would play Richard III.

About this time glowing accounts came of money to be made in Australia, and several of the Metropolitan stock actors left, and, headed by Booth and Anderson, formed themselves into a company for a professional tour of Australia and the Samoan and Sandwich islands. But dull times, affecting every kind of business, even the theater, had preceded them in Australia. Virtually penniless, they took return passage for San Francisco, where Booth found an engagement awaiting him at the Metropolitan.

Hard times soon decided Mrs. Sinclair to seek, in Sacramento, what promised better financial returns on her investments. She leased there a shabby little theater on a back street where she planned to produce outstanding plays. The venture was notable because there, in the dramatic season of 1855, was given the first performance in America of "The Marble Heart," and because Edwin Booth created in it the role of Raphael the sculptor.

Edwin now joined a company of actors assembled by one Moulton, which, with a brass band to cheer their way, played through the mountains and mining towns. The manager, his wife, the company, scenery, and wardrobe, and the band, traveled in a large wagon.

"The expedition," as described by William Winter, Booth's biographer, "met with intermittent public favour, but it was uniformly attended by one startling incident: each town took fire as soon as Moulton's cavalcade had left it, and so regularly did this lurid phenomenon recur that at last it became the theme of general remark, and Booth was known and designated as The Fiery Star. It was an epithet of ill-omen, but as a warning it was salutary. Ignorant and lonely communities are superstitious and dangerously impulsive. There was no obvious link between the strollers and the fires; but the logic of the mountaineers deduced the one from the other, and travel became unsafe for Moulton's caravan. At Downieville Booth found reason for solicitude as to his personal safety, and deemed it judicious to ride immediately out of town. The discreet manager, having private reasons to dread the sheriff, followed that example. Indeed, he improved upon it—for he ran away, not only from Downieville, but from his company. The band ceased to blow, the actors dispersed, the driver of the Moulton wagon seized Booth's horse, as security for money owed to him by the manager, and 'the fiery star' seemed to be quenched."

He returned to Sacramento penniless. Fortunately, a theatrical friend arranged a benefit for him, so that he was able to pay off all his debts before leaving for San Francisco. He was accompanied to the boat by a brass band from the theater and carried away with him a stickpin of California gold, representing a wrist and a hand, with a diamond between finger and thumb, a gift from the citizens. He remained a little while in San Francisco.

By September, 1856, an engagement awaited him in New York City, to play for the first time on Broadway. A brilliant farewell was tendered him.

In the *Daily Alta California* of September 4, under the heading "Farewell Benefit to Mr. Edwin Booth," appeared the following account:

"Mr. Booth appeared for the first time in one of the most arduous of Shakespeare's characters—King Lear—a part which the greatest actors have made the study of years, and one which requires a nicety of action, a thorough correctness in all the business of the stage, and a keen appreciation of the grandeur of the conception, for its successful representation. The figure of Mr. Booth is against him for the performance of such a character as Lear. In theatrical parlance, he is not 'heavy' enough for the part. After witnessing, however, his performance of Richelieu, which, next to that of Lear, we consider the finest 'old man's' part in the range of the drama, we were prepared to overlook the objections of face and form which militate against the successful representation of such characters by Mr. Booth. We were not prepared, however, for the complete triumph which he achieved over these objections in his performance of Lear. It was a triumph of art, and a triumph of which any actor on the stage might well be proud.

"The readings of Mr. Booth are very beautiful, and his style of acting pleasing and impressive; and, with care and study, we are satisfied he will yet become as great an actor as his father. In the 'curse scene,' in the first act, and in the 'mad scenes' he was particularly great, and throughout the whole performance exhibited more enlarged powers as an actor than we have ever given him credit for."

Booth sailed on the same steamer that had brought him to California in 1852 with his father. When he finally got back to the farm in Maryland, the weight of his trunk, heavy with books and belongings, greatly impressed the country lads who carried it. They whispered, with knowing winks, "He's from the diggin's." But Booth had carried away scarcely enough gold to pay his passage homeward.

He always gave due credit to San Francisco for that firm grounding in his art which he had gained here; but he never quite forgave her people for their tardy reward of his boyhood's passionate and faithful efforts—not even when, twenty years later, the city received him, to use his own words, "like a diva."

# 26

# The Opera

ONLY THE OPTIMISM of the pioneer and the speculative instincts of the gambler could have dared the financial risk involved in bringing opera to San Francisco. Fortunes were sunk in the first attempts to implant this achievement of Old World culture in a remote frontier town.

To those who thus dared, San Francisco owes much of its eminence in the musical world today. Whatever the shortcomings of the pioneer impresarios, they at least demanded the best that money could buy and the times and the conditions of transportation allow. The critics, on their part, showed the same daring independence of judgment that they had exhibited in their comments on the plays presented in the legitimate theaters.

To appreciate how hazardous the pioneer opera productions were, one must remember that the available theaters were liable to sudden destruction by fire, and that the price an impresario could charge for a seat was low. Indeed, the prices for admission, in proportion to what was charged for luxuries and for other recreations, and even for necessities, would, with few exceptions, be accounted low even in comparison with the prices of today.

San Francisco from the beginning had an overabundance of good music, both instrumental and vocal, available day and night, at the gambling "palaces." The first public concert, combined with recitations, was given at the old Post Office in Portsmouth Square, June 22d, 1849, by Steve Massett, the one-man show of the 'fifties. Four months later, October 22d, the Philadelphia Minstrels gave a performance at the Bella Union, with two dollars as the price of admission. Then—the first event approaching a matinee—the first public afternoon performance of an instrumental and vocal concert was given on January 5th, 1850, at the California Exchange. Later in 1850, Heinrich Herz, the renowned pianist, made his first appearance at the National Theater, the admission prices being six dollars for a box or a parquet seat and four dollars for a place in the pit. Herz was the first great pianist to come to San Francisco. At his concert there also appeared for the first time, as vocalist, the basso profundo, Signor Roncovieri, the father of a future superintendent of San Francisco's schools.

The National Theater had been opened, on the north side of Washington Street between Montgomery and Kearny, on February 19th, 1850, for French dramatic performances. It was destroyed by the fire of May 4th, less than four months later.

The following miniature pen picture of the arrival of the French Opera Troupe in San Francisco in the 'fifties is reproduced from a letter written by Signor Roncovieri to his wife in France, and now in the possession of his son.

"Let me tell you how we landed. We came ashore at four o'clock in the afternoon, bag and baggage. We inquired for lodgings, and were told that the rent of a single room, without furniture, would be five hundred francs—one hundred dollars—a month. So, to conserve our little funds as much as possible, we made a tent out of our bed sheets and camped on Telegraph Hill. We were perfectly comfortable. Then we started to work the next morning putting up the little 'knock-down' house that we brought with us. We found some more lumber here, and added a little lean-to kitchen in which we cook our meals, and which serves us as our dining room. So we live perfectly."

Following the French Opera Troupe came the Spanish Opera Company, to Foley's Olympic Circus. W. H. Foley had been a clown at Rowe's Olympic Circus until it was turned into Rowe's Amphitheater in the early part of February, 1850. After the fire of May, 1851, Foley purchased Rowe's site, resumed the name Olympic Circus, and inaugurated a series of bullfights. But this barbaric sport in the principal thoroughfare of San Francisco lasted but a fortnight. It was followed by the Spanish Opera Company, which opened on June 6th with ballet and scenes from various operas. Two weeks later a fire burned down the establishment, and the engagement came to a sudden end.

"The fire fiend," as a pioneer actor said, "played a pretty steady engagement in those days." In fact, he goes on, "illuminations had begun to be a habit with us, so that on one occasion during a juvenile concert comprising more than two hundred children the boys playfully kindled a bonfire on the place with about three hundred dollars' worth of oil belonging to the Manager, Thomas Maguire."

The first regular opera, by the first regular opera company, the Pellegrini Opera Troupe, opened at the Adelphi Theater, February 12th, 1851, with the first presentation in California of "La Sonnambula."

There were two Adelphi Theaters. The one in which this first opera was given was on the south side of Clay Street between Kearny and Montgomery. It was opened on November 9th, 1850, and was given over to dramatic performances. It, too, was destroyed by the fire of May 4th, less than six months from the day of its opening. A second Adelphi Theater was built on the west side of Dupont Street between Clay and Washington, and was opened by a French company on August 1st, 1851.

The Pellegrini Opera Troupe comprised seven members, three women and four men. Of these Signor Roncovieri appears as basso. Interwoven with the whole story of pioneer opera in San Francisco will be found the names of both Roncovieri and his wife. They appeared not only in French dramatic and musical companies, but in the Italian and English opera companies as well. Their son might be said to have been born in the theater. A pioneer scene-shifter tells me how he nursed him in the wings while his father, "a big, heavy-set fellow whose voice rattled the house," and his mother, "a little bit of a thing," were on duty behind the footlights.

Eight performances in all were given by this pioneer troupe—five performances of "La Sonnambula," two of "Norma," the first presentation of this opera in the State, as was also the single performance of "Ernani," which closed the season on April 8th. The price of admission for the first opera, "La Sonnambula," was four dollars for seats in the private boxes, three dollars for the dress circle, two dollars for the gallery, and one dollar for the second gallery.

After the fire of May, 1851, in which the original Adelphi Theater was destroyed, no record of opera appears again until the Planel French Opera Company opened for a season at the second Adelphi Theater on Dupont Street, on September 18th, 1853. This company consisted of eleven members, an increase of four over the first opera troupe. Monsieur Planel acted as conductor, his wife was the soprano, Madame Roncovieri the mezzosoprano, and Monsieur Roncovieri the basso.

In those days of slow travel and long distances, artists from "the States" who accepted a theatrical engagement in San Francisco usually came with their entire families; and the foreign artists brought not only their families, but all their household goods as well. Roncovieri came here, with four others, from Bordeaux, six months in advance of his wife. The journey covered twenty-five thousand miles, and consumed six months. Their original intention had been to make for the mines at French Gulch, where there was already a small colony of Frenchmen. They had a vision of a quick fortune to be made by picking up gold in the streets; the dull reality necessitated an adherence to their own less profitable profession.

The Planel French Opera Company gave, in all, five operas in fourteen performances, notably the first productions of "Le Barbier de Séville" and "La Fille du Régiment."

Just what either the first Italian opera company or the first French opera company left to be desired in the matter of voice, costumes, chorus, and presentation is recorded only indirectly, through the innuendoes implicit in the heralding of the coming of the first opera star, Madame Anna Thillon, with her English troupe. Yet the French and Italian troupes made at least sincere and earnest efforts to interpret the composers. This was more, it appears, than could be said of Madame Thillon, who seems to have been the embodiment of all the evils accompanying the pernicious star system of her time.

The Thillon English Opera Company came heralded as giving California, for the first time, "legitimate opera with a prima donna of acknowledged celebrity, with artists of high standing and undoubted merit in the other principal parts, with a chorus which could not be equaled anywhere for its effectiveness and great excellence, and with an orchestra made up of capable musicians, well drilled and under the leadership of George Loder, a gentleman who has scarcely a superior as a conductor in the United States. In addition, great care has been bestowed on the selection of the proper costumes, in the preparation of scenery and decorations, and in the procurement of such other accessories as are necessary to appropriate production."

Madame Thillon had an "acute, thin voice of marvelous timbre, with a range of two and a half octaves." She had had a career of "unclouded splendor" in Europe, and was "the pet of the composers, the pet of the public and the pet of the press." For more than two years "she had exercised sway over the music-loving portions of the people in the Eastern States."

The Thillon English Opera troupe opened at the new theater, the Metropolitan, January 16th, 1854, with "The Crown Diamonds," said to have been written expressly for Madame Thillon. The company comprised five members, among whom appears again the name of Roncovieri as basso. This company gave six operas in twenty-seven performances. Its season was notable for the first production in California of "The Bohemian Girl" and for the first production of French and Italian opera in English, much to the disgust of the Italian and French population, who expressed their opinion by a united refusal to attend.

Yet, notwithstanding the acclaim accorded to Madame Thillon by Europe and the East, the San Francisco musical critics refused to be blinded by the brilliancy of the star.

"Everything was cut out of the opera which could possibly divert the attention of the audience from Madame

Thillon," declared one critic. "She sang several arias and scenes, and that was all. She was the opera, and there was nothing of the work of the composer allowed to appear except just as much as was necessary to exhibit Madame Thillon."

This independent pioneer critic wrote as follows—and what present-day critic would dare write as boldy?—on Madame Thillon's farewell:

"Thillon makes up her paint and powder with forty years hid behind them. The beautiful mask of corked eyebrows, really fine eyes and teeth (how many had paternity in the dentist's office, the turnkey and forceps could better tell), her ringlets of beautiful purchased hair, her smiles manufactured to order, paddings well adjusted out of sight, and silks and satins worn tastefully, the possession of rare abilities as an actress and a fair voice well trained, gave her popularity and thirty thousand dollars in a short time in California. But she had nothing remarkable in the power, quality, compass, flexibility or finish of her voice. She was pretty on the stage, she sang fairly well, she had the advantage of long experience, and a youthful face and appearance carried long beyond youth's years, made, with the masses, all necessary atonement for any lack of the highest exhibition of musical genius. A large portion of her audience heard through their eyes, and let their ears pick up such crumbs of sound as came floating by."

In spite of the splendor of this shining first operatic luminary, opera did not become the habit necessary for the furtherance of musical art until the advent of Anna Bishop and Barili-Thorn, whose stepfather, Salvatore Patti, was the father of Carlotta, and of her sister, the great Adelina Patti.

The announcement of the arrival in town of the Barili-Thorn Italian Opera Company for an extended season at the Metropolitan was made on October 31st, 1854. Signora Barili-Thorn was the prima donna, Signor Scola the tenor, Lanzoni the baritone, and Bassani the director. With them, it was also announced, was Mlle. [Carlotta] Patti. Nothing was more propitious than the first night, when "Ernani" was produced. It was all that prices of from nine to twenty-five dollars for the private boxes could make fashionable and all that prices of three dollars for orchestra, two dollars for parquet and dress circle, and one dollar for the second and third galleries could make popular. Yet by May of the next year the company would have been happy in the possession of money enough for board and lodgings.

This engagement of the Barili-Thorn Italian Opera Company was significant, however, for two things: it established opera as a habit and a custom in San Francisco; and it marked the first public appearance of Carlotta Patti.

Carlotta was only fifteen; but so early a début was nothing for one of the Patti sisters; they had breathed the air of music from their infancy. Not only were their father and mother musicians of note; so also were their aunts and uncles, their half-brother Antonio, and their half-sister Clotilda Barili, who was married to Thorn, a man of some fortune. The mother, Caterina Barili, was a prima donna of the old school and a famous singer when she came to this country. Clotilda Thorn, and Antonio—who was long associated with Maurice Strakosch, the violinist, impresario, and only teacher of Adelina—were children of her first marriage. Patti the tenor, her second husband, was the father of Carlotta and Adelina.

Carlotta, who was three years the senior of Adelina, was a cripple. Had it not been for this defect, music critics say, she would have far outdistanced her famous sister in public acclaim. As it was, only the connoisseur preferred her to her sister. Because of her deformity, she sang only in concert, appearing always in front of a screen so placed that she could emerge from behind it without having to walk. She was more squarely built and lacked the oval beauty of face and coloring of Adelina, but her wit was more brilliant, her song more dashing and sparkling—possessed more *slancio,* as the Italians would say.

As a bravura singer, she is said to have had no peer. Adelina was a light soprano, who sang simple songs, always with exquisite sweetness, and everybody loved her. But where Adelina was loved, Carlotta was admired. She sang all the bravura airs with a dramatic and operatic manner that made her audience stand up and shout.

Carlotta's formal debut was made in New York in 1861, but her first public appearance was in this city, March 2d, 1855, in a pianoforte solo at the Metropolitan Theater on the occasion of the first production of "Lucia di Lammermoor" in Italian. This opera had been given in French, a short time before, by the Cailly French Opera Company, which was the Thillon troupe reorganized under a new management after the departure of Madame Thillon for a concert tour of the interior.

Carlotta also made her first appearance as a vocalist in this city on June 1st of the same year, at the Union Theater, singing Schubert's "Serenade." She began her career as a singer where most stars leave off. When a great operatic star, so I am told, begins to give concerts and sing oratorios, you may know his glory is on the wane; and at this point in his career he is sure to include in his repertoire Schubert's "Serenade."

Madame Barili-Thorn was more akin, in personal appearance at least, to her half-sister Adelina, possessing, according to the critic, "an exquisitely moulded form, a graceful motion, a queenly dignity, eyes large, dark and lustrous, arching brows, hair dark and abundant, and an enchanting smile that in an instant radiates her face like a sunbeam." But as a singer she was, according to the same critic, "cold and tame, finished and elegant rather than forcible, voice mezzo, of moderate register and volume, tone pure, thin, and uncertain, but of great excellence in the rendition of simple, beautiful music."

The Barili-Thorn Italian Opera Company played eight opera seasons, two of them in combination with the Anna Bishop company, and a third with the Montplaisir ballet troupe. The operas were, for the most part, those that had already been given in San Francisco in French and English.

They were now given in Italian. But the engagement was significant because it developed in the people the habit of going to the opera; and because, also, the musical talent of the city became concentrated into a musical stock company, and thus was laid the foundation that made it possible later for the great productions to come. San Francisco was too far distant from the metropolitan centers of the East to justify the transportation of an opera company with its entire cast; yet the great stars must be assured of some adequate support, and this the local stock company was able to give.

The Barili-Thorn company drew to its organization a number of artists who had come at different periods with the various companies and had remained to settle in the city: Madame von Gulpen, of the Pellegrini company, the first Italian opera company; Monsieur Planel, of the first French opera company; Roncovieri, and George Loder, who came as conductor to Biscaccianti, as well as other artists from the Bishop and Thillon companies.

By May the Barili-Thorn company had severed its connection with the Metropolitan in a row which was the spicy gossip of the city for a week. Public denunciations were hurled back and forth. Of these published statements I have been able to find but two, which I include, complete, for their rarity and because they are so representative of the spirit of the times. To the Company's statement that they refused to sing any longer for nothing, Mrs. Sinclair, Manager of the Metropolitan Opera Company, under date of

May 8th, 1855, replied, under the heading "The Italian Controversy," as follows:

Editor of the Herald: I beg to enclose to you the returns of the Treasurer of the Metropolitan Theatre of the receipts, expenses and losses attending the production of the Italian Operas, and as briefly as possible, with your permission, answer the card of Madame Thorn.

With regard to the profits made during Mr. and Mrs. Williams' [dramatic] engagement, I would simply state that reference is made to their first engagement preceding the appearance of the Italian Opera Troupe, and that all the money then made was subsequently lost by the operatic performances. In addition to the expenses enumerated by the Treasurer, I must add $332 for costumes furnished by me for Madame Thorn's use, some of which she still retains; likewise the nightly expense of a carriage to convey her to and from the Theatre.

No mention has been made of the serious losses accruing to the management from the subsequent postponements occasioned by Madame Thorn's illness, likewise Mr. Lanzoni's indisposition, on account of which "Don Giovanni" was put off after being announced. Since the date to which the Treasurer's account is made up, "Don Giovanni" was given twice, and for each representation Madame Thorn was paid $100. On the occasion of Mr. Lanzoni's benefit the charge of $700, as per agreement, was not made for rent alone (the rent of the Theatre being $100 per night), but for all the expenses of the Theatre, including the orchestra, etc. Up to this time Madame Thorn was paid in full, but I have never denied that some small arrears of salary are due to the other artists. The opera was repeated to a receipt of $150. I have never requested the artists to sing gratuitously, nor for my profit, and it was very evident that they were afraid to run any such risk when they declined trusting to a subscription, however complete its moral success.

I agreed to pay the artists a certain sum for the representation of "I Lombardi" on Tuesday, under the impression that great efforts would be used to secure a large house. At the rise of the curtain the receipts of the house amounted to $600, the disastrous commercial news received but a few hours before preventing the attendance of many persons. [The reference is to the great panic of 1855.]

Under the circumstances, I requested the Treasurer to send all the receipts to the artists, nothing being reserved for the Theatre. Of this sum, Madame Thorn received $300, the rest was divided among the artists and chorus, and I only learned the next day that no portion was appropriated to Mr. Planel. I think those engaged with me during more than eighteen months' management will uphold me in the assurance that I have never "duped" nor "injured" anyone. I have endeavored to the utmost of my ability to fulfill all my promises to the public; if on two occasions I have been prevented from doing so, it was because I could no longer derive from other sources the means of paying an Italian Opera Troupe more money than they drew to the treasury.

In justice to the gentlemen composing the orchestra and chorus, I should say that Mr. Loder [the conductor] informed me that they were ready to volunteer their services provided the artists would do likewise. In justice to Madame Bishop and Herr Mengis, I have forborne to make any mention of my arrangements with them, although they were for a time connected with the Italian Opera, but I would take occasion to say that at all times when called upon they have gratuitously sung for the benefit of all artists, native or foreign; that Madame Bishop never disappointed the public, and that she furnished all her own costumes, and did not require a carriage to take her from the International Hotel to the Theatre.

Praying you will pardon the inevitable length of this statement, I remain,

Most respectfully yours,
CATHERINE N. SINCLAIR.

Thus to money lost, as well as to money made and generously given to good causes, San Francisco owes a debt of thanks; to the grave of more than one lost fortune, a passing salute.

But there was another question of justice here. The Italian company replied, under date of May 10th:

EDITOR OF THE HERALD: The following is the reply of the Italian Opera Troupe to Mrs. Sinclair:

STATEMENT

*First Engagement* — *L. Bassani, Director*

*Receipts*

For sixteen representations (per account signed by Mrs. Sinclair) . . . . . . . . . . $18,392.00

The total divided as follows, viz.:

Proportion retained by Mrs. Sinclair (two-thirds) . . . . . 12,261.00

Proportion paid to Mr. Bassani (one-third) . . . . . . . . . . . 6,130.00

*Expenses*

The following defrayed by Mr. Bassani from his one-third, viz.: Salaries of Mde. B. Thorn, Messrs. Scola, Lanzoni, and others of the Italian Opera Troupe; salaries of Messrs. Laglaise, Roncovieri, Mengis, Leonardi, Loder; salaries of additional orchestra (three); and chorus (three); instructor of chorus music, costumes, and advertising in newspapers.

The following defrayed by Mrs. Sinclair from her two-thirds, viz.: Rent of theatre, lights, orchestra (nine, without leader), chorus (seven), figurantes and employés of the Theatre.

Nearly all the above composing the regular expenses of the Theatre, which was open on off nights with a dramatic company.

The public can judge from the foregoing what portion of the expenses was borne by Mrs. Sinclair, and will ask: In what consisted the expenses set down to her credit in the statement of the Treasurer at $21,902?

*Second engagement of the Italian Troupe and Madame Bishop and M. Bochsa—sole direction of Mrs. Sinclair*

From the "Expenses" of the management, according to the Treasurer's statement, should be deducted the following sums due to the artists:

| | |
|---|---|
| To Madame Barili-Thorn ($400 for benefit and $100 for a representation) | $500.00 |
| To Signor Scola | 250.00 |
| To Signor Lanzoni | 180.00 |
| To M. Laglaise | 110.00 |
| To M. and Mde. Roncovieri | 170.00 |
| To M. and Mde. Becherini | 125.00 |
| To Mr. Herold (leader) | 105.00 |
| To M. Planel | 160.00 |
| To chorus singers | 550.00 |
| To proprietor of costumes, music, etc. | 452.50 |
| | $2,602.50 |
| Add for rent of the Theatre, as appears by the proceedings in the Twelfth District Court, for the moiety of Mr. Trench, say | 8,800.00 |
| Total | $11,402.50 |

When the above sums are deducted from the "expenses" according to Mrs. Sinclair's statement, the real outlay of the house is reduced to a comparatively moderate amount, and the public will wonder how the entire profits of Mr. B. Williams' engagement can have been expended to support the opera troupe.

With regard to the "carriage," it was a part of the contract of engagement, and Madame Barili-Thorn then resided in Pike Street, and not at the International Hotel.

FOR THE ITALIAN OPERA.

After the departure of the Barili-Thorn company, the opera was not heard again until 1859, when the Bianchi Opera Company was imported by Tom Maguire.

# 27

# Tom Maguire

TOM MAGUIRE is said to have done more for the theater in San Francisco than any other one man. He and William T. Coleman, president of the Vigilance Committee, were considered the two handsomest men in the city.

Maguire was stocky of build, but had a soldierly bearing, a penetrating eye, a ruddy complexion, a heavy mustache, and a heavy head of hair. His hair, when it turned white, was like spun glass. He was always faultlessly attired, and was adorned with a big diamond in his scarf, a large solitaire on his finger, and a massive watch chain and charm across his waistcoat.

Every morning, about eleven o'clock, Maguire was a familiar sight on Washington Street, holding his levees on the curbstone in front of his theater.

Washington Street never slept; all night long, the lights, the music, and the voices, the clink of gold in gambling rooms, the charivari of the dance halls. At dawn came the restaurant and hotel men, for the early pick of produce just brought in. As the day advanced, stranger and citizen alike came to the Post Office and Custom House. And in the afternoon there came also the promenaders of the Ambrosial Path.

The banks and offices, mills and foundries, wholesale houses, retail shops, the big warehouses and auction rooms, the restaurants and theaters and fire-engine houses—all were within a few blocks of Maguire's. On Washington Street was Atwill's music store, the "hangout" of politicians and firemen, since Atwill himself was a politician and a great fire fighter. Directly across from Maguire's was the City Hall, Sam Sample's saloon, and Robert Tiffany's hat store.

The Snug, a "bit" saloon, with gambling rooms in the rear, was on the ground floor of Maguire's Opera House. Between acts, men from the audience came to gamble, entering by way of the saloon for a drink. The dealers, as was the custom of the time, went clad in long linen dusters and short black masks for the purpose of concealing their identity. Pistols being altogether too ready at that day, the dealer was in constant danger of his life through the rash act of some loser seeking vengeance.

On the same side as Maguire's, near Brenham Place, was Peter Job's, the "Sherry of the Pacific." Peter Job's was the best place in town for a French meal, for wedding parties and banquets, for fancy pastry and ice cream. The place was fitted up in Louis XIV style, with gilded chairs, silk hangings, and pier glasses hung between panels that were painted with Cupids among flowers. On Saturdays, Peter Job's was a favorite social rendezvous. The men came in ruffled shirts and frock coats, the women stiffly demure in high-laced bodices, their hoopskirts ballooning about them and tilting saucily up when they sat on the narrow gilded chairs to partake of the ice cream served in tall, narrow glasses.

Maguire had been a hackman in New York City. He came to San Francisco in 1849, and opened the Parker House as a gambling hall and saloon, with a theater, the Jenny Lind, on the floor above. Each time any of his theaters burned, straightway he rebuilt. Twice he rebuilt his Jenny Lind. In 1855, when he took over the San Francisco Hall of Minstrelsy, he at once built up the company by taking the pick of Christy's men and Billy Birch, the greatest "bones" of the period. In 1856 Maguire remodeled the building and changed its name to Maguire's Opera House.

Maguire's ambition was always to give the people of San Francisco the best theatrical talent available, and for many years no actor was too great to hire, nor his salary too high to pay. Maguire brought, at great cost, by way of the Isthmus and across the Plains, the greatest actors, the greatest spectacles, dramas, minstrels, and operas. As early as 1852 he induced the elder Booth to come. Nearly all the Shakespearean plays were produced at Maguire's theater. In all, twenty interpretations of "Hamlet" are said to have been presented there.

In 1857 Maguire imported Harry Courtaine and his wife, Emma Gratton, from London. Courtaine had achieved a reputation as a light comedian, notably as Captain Maidenblush in "The Little Treasure." It was when Courtaine was playing this role that James Nisbet, critic of the *Bulletin,* nearly broke the actor's heart by saying he was a "Jack pudding instead of a comedian." Nisbet's word was law—especially to Maguire; indeed, Maguire had such respect for Nisbet's judgment that whenever the critic *praised* an actor, whatever Maguire's own opinion might be, he called for the actor and raised his salary.

Courtaine had an elegant figure, and his movements on the stage are said to have been grace itself. He was an accomplished linguist and musician. He sustained with credit, in his prime, the roles of Figaro in "The Barber of Seville," and the Count in "Il Trovatore."

But Courtaine was notoriously a periodic drunkard, and at times, when he felt the spell upon him, he would lay aside his fine clothes and put on the rags of a tramp. He had been hardly a month in town when he was seized with one of his periodic thirsts. Maguire cut it short by locking Courtaine in jail; but the company, thinking him badly treated, bailed him out, whereupon he proceeded on his spree and Maguire vented his wrath on the Samaritans.

Courtaine remained in San Francisco upwards of twenty years. His life here was passed by turns on the stage, in the gutter, and in the county jail, where he used to serve his time out as a trusty. He occupied the same cell so often that it was called by his name. When at liberty, he accepted such brief engagements as he could find in the dives and melodeons. His early life was a mystery. In view of his many accomplishments, some credence was placed in the tale that he was the son of a dissolute Irish peer, the Marquess of Waterford.

Maguire built up not only a matchless minstrel company, but also a dramatic stock company. It included John McCullough, tragedian; Mrs. Saunders; Mrs. Judah, the character actress; Charles Thorne, "society villain"; Lucy Sweet; Mrs. Bowers; Sophie Edwin, who played in "East Lynne"; Frank Mayo, J. B. Booth, Jr., and David Anderson in old men's parts.

Frank Mayo, who had been employed in various minor capacities at Maguire's Opera House—peddling peanuts, captaining the supers, and the like,—suddenly became stage-struck. He succeeded in obtaining an engagement at the Metropolitan, his first appearance being that of the waiter in "Raising the Wind." Maguire then engaged him for small parts. Finally, he came to star in "David Crockett," a romantic play of frontier life. Such was his success in this play that he traveled the country with it for years.

Maguire brought out Edwin Adams, Joseph Jefferson, and Charles Kean, the English tragedian; Madame Céleste, the renowned French actress; and from Australia the dashing Lady Don, who made a splendid success in "Kenilworth." With Lady Don came Harry Edwards, as Mercutio in "Romeo and Juliet."

He imported the Bianchi Opera Company, the first complete Italian opera company, accompanied by the first "grand orchestra" (seventeen pieces in those days constituting a grand orchestra).

Eugenio Bianchi was a tenor almost without a peer at that time, and he introduced the pitch of the Paris Conservatory of Music to San Francisco. "At operas, between the acts," says August Wetterman, an orchestra conductor in this city since 1852, "Bianchi would come down to the music room with his tuning fork, the Paris Conservatory of Music pitch, which had been founded upon the human voice. He hit the fork on his knee, and then, holding it to our ears, would say, 'This is the right pitch. Gentlemen, you are all wrong. When I want to sing B flat, you force me to sing B natural. This is outrageous. You must change your pitch or you will kill me.' And we stood the abuse, knowing he was right."

Maguire imported the William Lyster English Opera Troupe, which gave operas in English, with Rosalie Durand as prima donna; also the Howison Opera Company, the Caroline Richings Opera Company, and Parepa Rosa.

Parepa Rosa was so fat that she looked like a bag tied round the middle, and because of the fat you couldn't see where it was tied. But when she opened her mouth it was as if the gates of Heaven were ajar. You forgot all about her fatness, and were only conscious of the sweetness, power, and wonder of her tone.

The bringing to San Francisco of Edwin Adams was considered a risky venture; but he proved indeed the "greatly beloved actor" of his time. He was a tragedian and emotional actor, notable for his impersonations of Hamlet and Enoch Arden, and of Robert Landry in "The Dead Heart." He fell a victim to consumption. At the benefit tendered him—it was a great success, bringing him $3000—the curtain disclosed him seated in a chair, for he was too weak to stand. He rallied a bit in the milder climate of San Rafael, where he lived some seven months. He returned East only to die.

Maguire brought out Edwin Forrest, and with him his leading man, John McCullough. Maguire expressed a desire to retain McCullough for his stock company. "You can't pay me what I can get in New York," said McCullough, not without a shade of contempt. "Who said anything about pay?" retorted Maguire. "How much do you want to stay?" McCullough demanded one hundred and fifty dollars a week—a fancy salary for stock—and Maguire agreed to pay it; so McCullough remained as leading man.

Maguire brought out Matilda Heron in "Camille," a play considered at that time quite *risqué*, for Matilda Heron, as has been noted earlier, followed the French school of interpretation. Maguire lost money on the venture, as he did also on "The Black Crook." For this play the bills announced Sallie Hinckley for the star part, and "an actual outlay of twelve thousand dollars for the original grand, romantic, magical and spectacular drama." The pulpits denounced "The Black Crook" even more roundly than they had "Camille." A pioneer sceneshifter has told me that for the Amazons in the grand march Maguire had to make a recruiting sergeant of every Madam in town; for to appear in tights was considered *infra dig*. even for a showgirl.

Tom Maguire, I am told, was never happy in any venture unless it had some element of risk. He was a born gambler. However heavy his loss, he was always ready to take another big chance. It was this that made him first in most things theatrical—the first to bring out the great Booth, the great Forrest, the great plays. He was the first to bring out a Japanese troupe of acrobats. Once, when Maguire went broke, "Lucky" Baldwin staked him to the Baldwin Theater, where Maguire, with the true gambler's spirit, backed Salmi Morse's "Passion Play"—and lost.

Goldstein the costumer pronounced this play the most "sublime and beautiful" ever put on in this city. But public sentiment and an ordinance of the Supervisors declared it "indecorous and damaging to religious sentiment." James O'Neill, the Jesus of the original cast, Lewis Morrison, the Pontius Pilate, David Belasco, and other members of the Baldwin Stock Company, were haled into the Police Court and fined. After a second performance, at the Grand Opera House, in deference to public opinion the play was withdrawn. Salmi Morse, the author, who had intended only the pure and elevating, in his grief at this complete misunderstanding, committed suicide.

Maguire usually had two theaters going at one time in San Francisco—his Opera House, owned and controlled solely by himself, and the Metropolitan which he and John

Torrence jointly leased. Later he replaced the Metropolitan venture with his Academy of Music, which he built himself and designed principally as a temple for grand opera.

"Maguire's one besetting sin," in the words of Johnny Ryan, once a Maguire callboy, "was the love of grand opera. In those days the taste of the people did not run to high-class entertainment, but Maguire insisted upon getting the very best. Events proved that Maguire could make more money out of a season with Alice Kingsbury in "Fanchon the Cricket," or Billy Birch's Minstrels, than he could with a dozen Brambillas, Mancusis, and Parepa Rosas put together; still, he would have them, and many a season left him broke—but not discouraged."

Maguire brought whole opera companies from the East, and paid them lavishly. He plunged with salaries of $1000 a night for a star and $250 a week for a man who could supply his own costumes, Maguire not wishing to go to the trouble of providing costumes as the contract stipulated. On a four months' season of the Adelaide Phillips Italian Opera he lost $30,000.

On one occasion, however, it is recorded that he broke even. He had sent his Caroline Richings Opera Company on a tour. They arrived at Virginia City for a night's performance, and found the whole town flocking to the circus. But early in the evening a storm came up, blowing down the circus tent and sending the people rushing to the theater, not only for shelter, but also because it was the only other place in town to see a show.

# 28

# Minstrels

SAN FRANCISCO'S social beginnings were sadly handicapped because the ladies would not venture forth—the omnipresent mud and the high cost of fashionable dress made them hesitate. To hear and see a renowned actor or singer, a few of them might overcome their reluctance. Biscaccianti, indeed, had succeeded in attracting them to concerts, and for a while they had attended plays and operas; but with the departure of the Barili-Thorn Italian Opera Company there came a slump both in music and the legitimate drama. The town had been surfeited with attractions. Once more the streets, the theaters, and social affairs presented a "monotonous scene of breeches."

Some enterprising individuals, in a burst of optimism and enthusiasm for San Francisco's social welfare, attempted a series of "promenade concerts."

"A large crowd was present on the first evening, but, unfortunately for the managers, there were no ladies present to join in the ball at the close of the concert; and such a scene as was presented when the dancing commenced beggars description.

"The large hall was crowded with that portion of the community who wear boots and hats. The music commenced; it was a polka; but no one liked to venture. At last two individuals, evidently determined to start the thing, ladies or no ladies, grappled each other in the usual way, by the shoulder, waist, and hands, and commenced stumping it through the crowd and around the hall. An oval track was soon left for them, and as they passed successive portions of the crowd their efforts were accompanied by laughter, ironical applause, and shouts of 'Good boy!' 'Put in the big licks, old fellow!' 'There you go with yer eye out!'

"Nothing daunted, however, they continued their terpsichorean endeavors with a pair of sober faces. They were soon joined by another couple, who ventured amid cries of 'Brava!' and at last three or four more added to the amusement, all persevering until the music ceased.

"The *tout ensemble*—the measured cadence of thick-toed soles as these double planets struck out from the chaotic mass of men, revolved about their axis and around the oval orbit, appearing, passing by the field of observation, and disappearing, one after the other, the ballroom filled with laughing men, and the really excellent orchestra playing as earnestly as though the room were filled with ladies of state and the ball had been opened by Prince Albert himself—was amusing in the extreme.

"The next dance was a cotillion, and, two-thirds in joke, enough joined in to make four sets, who took their places at the head of the hall, the remainder of the company retiring a certain distance so as to leave ample space for that portion of the mass which had resolved itself into order.

"The music struck up, most obsequious bows were made, each one placing the crown of his hat in such a position that a full view of it would have been presented to his partner, had the latter not bowed also, and the cotillion was in general conducted with great propriety.

"When the 'balances' came, however, the different couples acted like wild comets, erratically striking off and far into the black-coated chaos of spectators, to the great detriment of the several toes thereof and the vegetable protuberances thereon. All was taken in good part, however, and when the music ceased there was uproarious applause. As dance after dance was announced, more and more joined in, until, in an hour or two, nearly the whole chaotic mass had resolved itself into order.

"It was the most unique affair ever witnessed—a large and splendid hall, brilliantly lighted, a very small orchestra discoursing most excellent music, and the whole floor covered with cotillions composed entirely of men, with hats on, balancing to each other, chassezing, everyone heartily enjoying the exhilarating dance, and no less enjoying the palpable humor of the scene, of which each conspired to form a part.

"We have witnessed in a ballroom one single 'stag cotil-

lion,' but never until last night had we seen a v
covered with them, as thick as they could stand.
actually a species of sublimity in the 'stag-ishn
scene. One would think, too, there would have b
of confusion as the night waned and the company became excited, but, strange to say, such was not the fact.

"It is true, the musicians attempted to pack their instruments before the dances designated on the cards had all been played, and that this was a signal for great indignation and shouting and a precipitate rush for the platform, where a small scene of broken music stands and 'chairs *volantes*' occurred. But soon sundry bottles of champagne appeared for the benefit of the musicians, whereat said musicians were conciliated and pacified, the music recommenced, order was restored, the dancing went on with as great propriety as though the room were crowded with ladies and finally, an hour before daylight, the entertainment closed, each wending his way quietly, or otherwise, to his lonely bachelor room."

McCabe, in his diary, records briefly the demise of this brilliant idea:

"September 1 [1854]—Promenade concert announced, Musical Hall, but a failure, no ladies attending.

"September 3—Closing night of nightly promenade concerts, Musical Hall."

But soon a kind and quality of entertainment offered that did bring the ladies out *tout à fait*—it was Christy's Minstrels.

Minstrel performances had been given in San Francisco before this. As early as October 22d, 1849, the Philadelphia Minstrels had appeared at the Bella Union. The Pacific Minstrels were announced for an opening performance on December 24th of the same year, which, however, was prevented by a large fire in the city. The Virginia Serenaders played in 1850, at Washington Hall. The Sable Harmonists came in 1851, playing in the interlude of the bill at the first Jenny Lind Theater, January 15th to 19th, and on February 22d to 28th giving a full performance. On February 25th "a large company honored these delightful harmonists."

But Negro minstrelsy did not become a permanent institution until Christy, in October, 1854, sent part of his troupe to San Francisco under the direction of Tom Briggs the banjoist. Christy, who had been making big money in New York and abroad, saw still bigger money to be made in the gold excitement of California; so he split his company, sending one-half to this coast.

The cast included some of his greatest stars: E. O. Christy, who made a specialty of Stephen Foster's songs; Eph Horn, famous end man and general all-around comedian; Dan Bryant, who achieved lasting fame in his dance, "Essence of Old Virginny," and his delineations of the hungry Negro in "Old Time Rocks"; S. C. Campbell, baritone; I. Donniker, "leader"; Mairs, wench dancer; Pierce, one of the greatest minstrel comedians of his day; and lastly, Thomas F. Briggs, the white banjoist, pupil of that master of the banjo, Sweeny the Virginia Negro. He had invented the banjo thimble and he was the first to do bell chimes and imitations of horse racing on his instrument. Some say he had consumption before he left the East; others, that he contracted the Isthmus fever on the voyage. At all events, on October 24th, 1854, the day following the opening performance, he died.

The loss of Tom Briggs completely demoralized the company. Christy returned East in December, taking with him Donniker, Mairs the wench dancer, and Pierce.

On the heels of their departure, Jerry Bryant, who had struck up a boon companionship with Orrin Dorman, one of the proprietors of the Bank Exchange saloon, induced Dorman to sell out his interest to John Torrence and go in for what promised to be a fortune in the minstrels. Dorman, together with Dr. Robinson, Torrence, and Jerry Bryant, took over San Francisco Hall and filled out the remnant of Christy's famous band with an equal number of picked stars of the Backus Minstrels. On January 23d, 1855, the company, with Dorman as manager, opened under the style of the Christy-Backus Minstrels. On January 29th the name was changed to the San Francisco Minstrels, and under that name the company has gone down in history.

The people went wild. The hall was crowded nightly. The problem that had vexed men's hearts and taxed their ingenuity for several years was solved in the twinkling of an eye: the ladies became even more enthusiastic than the men. Every one of them *had* to go to the minstrels, fine clothes or no, mud or no mud, fair weather or foul.

# 29

## Melodeons

IN CONTRAST to theaters dedicated to the legitimate drama, or, like the San Francisco Hall of Minstrelsy, boasting of "female attendance," were the melodeons—a word used to signify houses playing exclusively to "stag audiences."

The melodeons were variety theaters, or, as at Gilbert's Melodeon and the Bella Union, gave variety performances in conjunction with minstrelsy. But where the San Francisco Hall of Minstrelsy begged to inform the public of the "chaste order" of its performances, "nightly visited by the élite and fashion" and "numerous female attendants," Gilbert's Melodeon bid for favor by advertising its "freedom from constrained etiquette."

In the melodeons, women were permitted only as performers or as waitresses to sell drinks. The waitresses were honest hired help. They were not exploited as an attraction until much later, when vulgar performances were introduced. This was essentially true of the Bella Union Melodeon. Under the regime of its founder, Samuel Tetlow, the entertainments were at times ultrasensational, but he also put on such plays as "Dombey and Son," a weepy dramatic version, by James A. Hearne, of Dickens' well-known story. In illustration of this difference between the earlier period and the later decadence I give on these pages two excerpts from show bills, one by Tetlow and the other by Ned Foster, proprietor of the Bella Union in the 'nineties.

[Tetlow's bill]

NIGHTLY

A CONSTANTLY VARIED ENTERTAINMENT

Replete with FUN and FROLIC
Abounding in SONG and DANCE
Unique for GRACE and BEAUTY
Wonderful ECCENTRICITY
Extraordinary for its NOVELTY
And Perfect in Its Object of Affording
LAUGHTER FOR MILLIONS!
in which
HARRY COURTAINE
Sally Thayer, Maggie Brewer, Sam Wells, J. H. O'Neill, William Lee, J. Allen, Marian Lee, Nellie Cole, A. P. Durand, J. H. McCabe, C. Staderman, Amanda Lee, Ellie Martell, H. D. Thompson, Joe Mabbot, T. M. Wells, G. Woodhull and a Host of the Best
DRAMATIC, TERPSICHOREAN and MUSICAL TALENT WILL APPEAR
Emphatically the
MELODEON OF THE PEOPLE
Unapproachable and Beyond Competition!

[Foster's bill]

FULL-GROWN PEOPLE
Are invited to visit the
BELLA UNION
If they want to "Make a Night of It."
The Show is Not of the Kindergarten Class,
but Just Your Size if You Are
Inclined to be Frisky and Sporty.
It is Rather Rapid, Spicy and Speedy—As
Sharp as a Razor, and as Blunt at Times
as the Back of an Ax. At the
BELLA UNION
You will find
PLAIN TALK and BEAUTIFUL GIRLS!
REALLY GIRLY GIRLS!
No Back Numbers, but as Sweet and Charming
Creatures as Ever Escaped a Female
Seminary.
Lovely Tresses! Lovely Lips! Buxom Forms!
at the
BELLA UNION
and Such Fun.
If You Don't Want to Risk Both Optics,
SHUT ONE EYE.
As for the Program, That Is Enough to Make
a Blind Man See—It Is an
EYE-OPENER.
We Could Tell You More About It, but It
Wouldn't Do Here. Seeing is Believing and
If You Want Fiery Fun and a Tumult-
uous Time—Come to the
BELLA UNION THEATER

The most popular melodeons at the time when Kearny Street was widened (the city, by this time, had become alive with them) were Gilbert's, Bert's New Idea, the Olympic, and the Bella Union. At Gilbert's, in the late 'fifties, Joe Murphy, Lew Rattler, Johnny de Angelis (father of the later well-known Jefferson de Angelis), and Lotta held sway. But the most imposing numbers of dramatic and variety stars were cradled at the Bella Union—a list so long that only the foremost can be mentioned: James A. Hearne, dramatic actor; Charles Reade, of minstrel fame; Tommy Bree, famous banjoist; Patti Rosa, soubrette, and Fannie Young, dramatic actress; Pauline Markham, burlesque star; Tom Caselli, singer; Sam Rickey, Charles McCarthy, and Bobby Gaylor, Irish comedians; and Ned Harrigan.

One of the greatest favorites of the Old Bella Union was Ned Harrigan, who in after years, in partnership with Tony Hart, established Harrigan & Hart's in New York, the home for many years of local dramas dealing with New York life, such as "The Mulligan Guards," "Squatter Sovereignty," and "The Leather Patch."

Ned Harrigan was a ship caulker, making his five dollars a day in Vallejo, when he became stage-struck and applied at Gilbert's Melodeon. He lasted three days. Ned Buckley, stage manager of the Bella Union, who for nine years previously had been end man and bones in the position left vacant by Joe Murphy, encountered Harrigan, looking rather forlorn, standing in the rain in front of Alex McKenzie's saloon, and asked him what was his trouble. On Harrigan's asking if Buckley could get him work at the Bella Union, he went to Madame Tetlow and told her that in order to make the show complete they should have a comic singer, and recommended Ned Harrigan for the place. At first she was unwilling to increase expenses, but Buckley was insistent. She asked what Harrigan would come for; Buckley answered, twenty-five dollars; she could not think of paying more than eighteen; the bargain was closed for twenty.

Buckley hastened back to Harrigan and told him to organize his Vallejo friends and have them come to the opening performance. At rehearsal the leader of the orchestra, after trying Harrigan in different keys, gave up in despair, saying, "Mr. Buckley, it isn't in the fiddle." But by night detachments began to come in from Vallejo, friends of Harrigan's caulker days, nine at a time, asking if "Harrigan the singer" was to appear. Then came a batch of ten, followed shortly by twenty, all putting the same inquiry to Madame Tetlow. In all, Harrigan marshaled a hundred and fifty friends that night. Madame Tetlow remarked to Buckley that "that fellow Harrigan certainly had a lot of friends."

Although Harrigan had a deficient ear, from the start he showed an ability to win an audience. Before he left the Bella Union, a year later, his salary had risen to fifty dollars a week, an unusual sum in those days for a variety actor.

Madame Tetlow was the business end of the concern. She engaged the talent, making the best bargains she could, and being a shrewd woman she rarely got the worst of it. She also sold tickets. Not until late years did the Bella Union have a box office; the theater was entered either through the saloon or by a long, narrow hallway at the end of which

Madame Tetlow sat at a table and sold admissions. When the new Bella Union was built in 1868, this same entrance arrangement was preserved.

The Bella Union, as we have seen, started as a gambling den in 1849. But it had an auditorium with chairs about. When, in 1856, gambling was done away with, Samuel Tetlow took advantage of this auditorium to erect a stage and give variety performances at twelve and a half cents admission.

Tetlow was a unique character. He is said to have had the finest collection of gold nuggets in San Francisco. He used to enjoy his own shows as much as any deep-sea sailor with whom he was wont to sit in the boxes and witness the performances. He did not know beforehand what was going to be produced, as he gave free rein to his stage manager.

The Bella Union at this time gave the greatest variety entertainment in the United States, a statement borne out by the programs, one of which I offer here. So great became its fame that every sailor the world over considered his stay at San Francisco incomplete without a visit to the Bella Union—just as every bride considered marriage incomplete without asking her husband if he had ever been to the Bella Union, and if so, why, and what it was like.

Much, too, of the greatness of these shows arose from the fact that San Francisco was far from the center of supply for variety theaters, so that, when performers came West they were engaged for never less than four weeks, and often for a whole season or a year, if they showed versatility.

WEDNESDAY EVENING, MAY 7TH, 1862

PART FIRST

Medley Overture and Chorus (Composed by Mr. J. Allen).... BY THE COMPANY
Silver Midnight Winds.......... MISS ELLIE MARTELL
Cheer, Boys, Cheer.......... SAM WELLS
Jane Munroe.......... SALLIE THAYER
Shells of Ocean.......... JOE MABBOTT
Jenny is My Darling.......... MISS MAGGIE BREWER
The Dumb Wife.......... MARIAN LEE
Operatic Chorus.......... COMPANY

To Conclude With a
MEDLEY WALK AROUND
Introducing Billy Patterson, Daro Aro, Johnny Roach, Barkeep, Jenny Comb Your Hair, Nigger in the Tent, etc. by the Company.
And J. H. O'Neill's Celebrated Imitations of Preceding Dancers.

WONDERFUL FEAT OF BALANCING ON A SINGLE WIRE
M'LLE ELLA CADEZ

Song and Dance.......... J. H. O'NEILL
Ballad.......... MAGGIE BREWER
Favorite Dance.......... AMANDA LEE
The Emigrant.......... JOE MABBOTT
Somersault Reel and Jig.......... A. P. DURAND

To be followed by the Glorious Farce of
SIAMESE TWINS

Mr. Forceps, a Virtuoso.......... MR. MCCABE
Captain Vivid.......... T. M. WELLS
Dennis O'Glib } Siamese Twins.......... { SAM WELLS
Simon Slow } { H. D. THOMPSON
Marian, ward to Forceps.......... NELLIE COLE
Sally.......... SALLIE THAYER

Ballad.......... MAGGIE BREWER
Double Irish Jig.......... LEE AND J. H. O'NEILL
Ballad.......... ELLIE MARTELL
Solo and Variations, "Sandy Boy," showing the different modes of playing the Violin.......... J. ALLEN
The Shamrock Green.......... JOE MABBOTT

TERRIFIC ASCENSION!
From the STAGE to the GALLERY, WITHOUT A BALANCE POLE! on a SINGLE WIRE!.......... M'LLE ELLA CADEZ

To Conclude with
A COUNTRY DANCE
By the Company

ADMISSION.......... 12½ CENTS
Parquette.......... 25 Cts. Orchestra Seats.......... 50 Cts.
Curtain rises at 8 o'clock precisely.

All actors engaged for the Bella Union, as well as for other variety theaters of the time, contracted not only to do their specialties, but also to appear in opening acts, afterpieces, and dramas when they were needed.

Samuel Tetlow's proprietorship of the Bella Union ended in July, 1880, when he shot and killed his partner, Billy Skeantlebury, in the saloon—over business matters, it is said. He was acquitted, on a plea of self-defense. His wife died. He fell a victim to the wiles of a blonde chorus girl, and ended his days in poverty.

Tragedy was the early heritage of the Bella Union. In 1849 Reuben Withers killed Reynolds there. Frank Hussey, a minstrel, accidentally killed his best friend, Tom Raleigh, while attempting to frighten, with a loaded revolver, a drunken man who was disturbing the performance. Lotta was playing at the Bella Union at the time. Elias Lipsis, an actor at the Bella Union, said to be a half-brother of Adah Isaacs Menken, committed suicide from jealousy of his wife, Carrie, an actress. Tommy Tuers, champion flatfoot dancer, killed James Dowling, the stage manager, when both were employed there. He was acquitted and went to raising pigs out Colma way.

With all the thousands of dollars made, no manager ever left the Bella Union with a competency. Almost everyone "went broke." The fortunes of the house went from bad to worse; it is last remembered as the Eden Musée, with wax-works in the rear and a penny arcade in front, all burned in the fire of 1906.

# Index